THE MAN GOD USES

By

E. A. JOHNSTON

COVER PHOTO:

Author is seen standing on Whitefield's Tump, Minchinhampton Common where George Whitefield preached to 20,000 in open air

DEDICATION

THIS BOOK IS DEDICATED WITH WARM AFFECTION TO MY DARLING DAUGHTER CARLY, OF WHOM I AM PROUD OF THE WOMAN SHE HAS BECOME THROUGH THE ADVERSITY SHE HAS FACED.

E. A. Johnston
November 2024

"Whenever I get too big for my britches, God puts me on His grill and barbecues me!" E. A. Johnston

TABLE OF CONTENTS

8

INTRODUCTION

When God gets ready to do something He sends a man to a people—a man sent from God. God is looking for a man to use for His purpose. We see from the Word of God:

> *"For the eyes of the LORD run to and fro throughout the whole earth, to show himself strong in the behalf of them whose heart is perfect toward him"* (2 Chronicles 16:9).

God is uncovering every stone and searching in every place to find that man that He can use. Often a man used by God is a man set apart for God, consecrated to God, and wholly given to God. This was true in the life of D. L. Moody. Before Moody was well known as an evangelist, he was in England sitting on a park bench speaking with a minister who said to him, "Moody, the world has yet to see what God can do with the man wholly sold out to Him." Moody walked away from that meeting, muttering under his breath—"Oh God! Make me that man!" And God did just that!

For a man to be used of God there must first be a desire on the man's part to be used of God. A man not only willing to be used of God but wholly given to and surrendered to God! *"Whose heart is perfect toward him."* Our text declares. He must be a man of God on fire for God and useful to God. What makes a man useful to God? That will be the subject for our treatise on "The Man God Uses."

If you have a desire to go deeper with God and be more useful to Him then this book is for you friend. But bear in mind there will be a sacrifice to be made. For what costs counts and what counts costs. May God grant you the grace to become more useful to Him for the good of His people and the glory of His name!

CHAPTER ONE:
THE MAN GOD USES:
IS A MAN OF PRAYER

- ❖ "I was lost and Jesus found me, I was filthy and He cleansed me,
- ❖ I was a rebel and He conquered me, I was crooked and He straightened me,
- ❖ I was empty and He filled me,
- ❖ I was broken and He used me."

E. A. Johnston

I used to live in a forest, and I had to build a long fence around my property to keep wild animals out. I had a dog and a little daughter who played in the back yard and that fence was built for protection and safety to keep out bobcats, coyotes, and the occasional wolf. But we'd get some bad storms in the spring every year and the force of wind and water would break down the fence and bust a hole in it. I would have to get some wood, and some heavy stones and load them in a wheelbarrow to repair that fence line. I would stack those heavy stones atop one another to fill up the hole or gap made by the storm and I did this to keep the danger out.

In Ezekiel chapter twenty-two and verse thirty we read:

"And I sought for a man among them, that should make up the hedge, and stand in the gap before me for the land, that I should not destroy it: but I found none."

Here is a picture of a broken-down hedge with imminent danger lurking near it, ready to break it at any moment with ruin and destruction. It is a picture of a provoked God by His sinful, rebellious people and He wants to extend mercy and not destroy them but He is missing something; missing someone. A man. An intercessor. If only an intercessor would make up the hedge and stand in the gap by desperate prayer, then God would relent and not destroy. In this case, "standing in the gap" not for a person but a nation.

So here in our text God is looking for a man. Is He looking for a Prince? A Statesman? A military general? No. Our text says, "a man." But not just any man will do. But a man suitable to the task. A special man with a certain specialty in prayer—an intercessor. He is the only one who can stand in the gap and be effective and get the job done. So the man God is looking for is a Man of Prayer.

We have a more detailed description of him over in the Book of James. Let's turn there now to James chapter five and in verses fifteen to seventeen, to learn more about this man. We pick up our description of him in the middle of verse sixteen where we read,

> *"The effectual fervent prayer of a righteous man availeth much."*

So first and foremost, a righteous man is needed. This means one who is born again and in a right relationship with God. A man of God who walks with God. Amos 3:3 declares,

> *"Can two walk together, except they be agreed?"*

The answer is "no." One must be in a close relationship with God to walk with God. Friends must be in agreement to be friends. God is looking for a man sold out to Him who desires more of Him.

The kind of man needed for the task of standing in the gap is a righteous man. But what kind of prayer is needed? Let's take a look: our text in James which says *"The effectual fervent prayer of a righteous man."* Effectual denotes one who is active and energetic. Fervent prayer is burdened, broken, sacrificial prayer. Prayer that costs something. There is a sacrifice involved—the sacrifice of time and wrestling in agonizing prayer. What costs counts and what counts costs. The word "fervent" in the Greek signifies prayer that is inspired by the Holy Ghost. It's the inspired prayer of a righteous man wrought by the operation of the

Holy Ghost. We see mention of this kind of praying in Jude 1:20,

> *"But ye, beloved, building up yourselves on your most holy faith, praying in the Holy Ghost."*

For to pray in the Holy Ghost means you first must be anointed by the Holy Ghost and filled with the Holy Ghost. For to pray in the power of the Spirit means unobstructed access to the Almighty, influence to gain His attention and power to attain answers to our pleading petitions. For praying in the Holy Ghost storms the portals of heaven with a holy violence, and makes fire fall upon the drenched altar of sacrifice; it makes kings tremble and kingdoms shake. For a man praying in the power of the Holy Ghost can startle the very angels in heaven and rattle the red-hot gates of hell! For a man full of the Spirit and anointed with the Spirit and praying in the Spirit knows no resistance, has no opposition, fears no earthly mortal and conquers all unearthly enemies.

Additionally, we read in James 5:17&18,

> *"Elijah was a man subject to like passions as we are, and he prayed earnestly that it might not rain; and it rained not on the earth by the space of three years and six months. And he prayed again, and the heavens gave*

rain, and the earth brought forth her fruit."

The expression, "prayed earnestly" infers supplication to God for a particular benefit; either the supplication or intercession on the behalf of an individual, who perhaps is sick, and the prayer is for healing; or it may be intercession on the behalf of a nation that it might not be destroyed. A sinful nation that has turned its back on God and deserves judgement. Like Moses stood in the gap for the Israelites who sinned against God with the golden calf in an out and out orgy! In Exodus 32:11-14, we have a pattern for intercessory prayer in how Moses pleaded with the Lord on behalf of the people:

"And Moses besought the LORD his God, and said, LORD, why doth thy wrath wax hot against thy people, which thou hast brought forth out of the land of Egypt with great power and with a mighty hand? Wherefore should the Egyptians speak, and say, For mischief did he bring them out, to slay them in the mountains, and to consume them from the face of the earth? Turn from thy fierce wrath, and repent of this evil against thy people. Remember Abraham, Isaac, and Israel, thy servants, to whom thou swarest by thine own self, and saidst

unto them, I will multiply your seed as the stars of heaven, and all this land that I have spoken of will I give unto your seed, and they shall inherit it forever. And the LORD repented of the evil which he thought to do unto his people."

So, Moses here prayed fervently and earnestly making supplication on the behalf of a people in intercessory prayer. We should do the same. Is our nation evil? Has not our nation turned its back on God? Has not our nation called evil good and good evil? Why doesn't God destroy us? There are those who make up the hedge and stand in the gap—that person can be you! God is not looking for a superhero but a man—the right man for the job.

James says that Elijah was a man subject to like passions as we are. Elijah was an imperfect man who believed in a perfect God and leaned on that God in prayer by faith and he got the job done as an intercessor. God is looking for that kind of man today! A man of prayer! Not in casual prayer or occasional prayer but desperate prayer and fervent prayer! But there is a cost involved in being an intercessor.

For a prayer life that grips the attention of the heavenly throne room is not built beneath calm, sunny skies but shaped during dark sorrow-filled nights. A serious prayer life is hammered out on the anvil of pain and affliction, desperation and despair, when hope hangs on a tattered thread and all human resources are gone. There and only there does the answer to the request come. Here is where the vital prayer life commences which gains the cupped ear of the Almighty, as He leans over to listen more intently to the pathetic sobs and anguished heart-cries; which in desperation reach out for His robe of righteousness to grab hold of and hang onto and not let go like Jacob wrestling with the Angel until the blessing is attained. To become a person of prayer is to be a shrill, holy note which continually rings the ears of angels, and pounds on the gates of glory! A true prayer life is born out of necessity: in your leanness you will learn to lean on Him. Through your rolling on stormy seas, you will be enabled to roll it all onto Him. When friends fail, disappoint and desert you, you will seek and find favor with your Faithful Friend Jesus.

> *"And I sought for a man among them that should make up the hedge and stand in the gap before me, for the land that I should not destroy it."*

Friend, will God find you standing there?

Let us pray, "Great God! You are holy and the Ancient of Days! Forgive us for our multiplied sins as a people. We have forsaken Thee and turned our backs on Thee. We have banned You from our school house; legislated You out of the Court House; kicked You out of the White House; and locked You out of the Church House. We are a spiritually bankrupt people who deserve judgment from on High. I pray in Your wrath, remember mercy. In Your wrath, remember mercy! Send us a mighty revival and spiritual awakening to our land that will grip this generation of young people and shake this nation from coast to coast! I pray these things in the strong name of Jesus! Ahmen!"

The man God uses is a man of prayer.

CHAPTER TWO

THE MAN GOD USES:
IS A MAN OF FAITH

❖ "Faith is standing on the promises of God when there
❖ is nothing left to stand on."

E. A. Johnston

In Hebrews 11:6 we read,

"But without faith it is impossible to please him: for he that cometh to God must believe that he is, and that he is a rewarder of them that diligently seek him."

Years ago I had a heart burden to go deeper with God in my walk with Him. I asked God to make me a man of faith. At the time I did not properly understand what a man of faith was but I knew God would honor that request and make me a man of faith—from His perspective. Little did I realize at the time what would have to transpire in my life to make that prayer a reality in my life. There would be deep waters I would have to pass through, hardships I thought I never would have to encounter, and trials and losses which, had I known in advance what they were, I would have shied away from my request for

God to make me a man of faith. But in the providence of God He knew the most effective means to use in my life to strip away what was hindering His work in my life and to burn out the dross in me that needed to go out so more of Christ could come in.

The faith life is the most exciting adventure in the world! The man that God uses is a man of faith. Faith has to be developed by the spiritual eyes rather than the physical because one must see beyond his circumstances to see God at work. I believe faith and obedience go hand in hand like biscuits and gravy: for in Hebrews 5:7-9 we read:

> *"Who in the days of his flesh, when he had offered up prayers and supplications with strong crying and tears unto him that was able to save him from death, and was heard in that he feared: though he were a Son, yet learned he obedience by the things which he suffered: and being made perfect, he became the author of eternal salvation unto all them that obey him."*

For God to answer my prayer and make me a man of faith He had work to do in me and that wasn't going to happen all at once or overnight. It would take years to make this desire a reality in my life. Moses had much of Egypt still in him when he fled from Pharoah to go to the Midian desert. It took God forty years on the backside of the desert to get all of Egypt out of Moses. We read the comments of F. J. Heugal who wrote:

> "For forty years on the lonely slopes of Midian the fiery Moses is schooled. There were graves, if I may so speak, scattered all over the mountainside where hope after hope was buried until at last, self went down in utter annihilation."

I had a lot of the world in me that God had to get out of me before He could build me into a man of faith from His perspective. And through the years as God was developing faith in me, He would give me incredible instances of His presence and power and supernatural activity in my life that would increase my faith and strengthen my faith. As Jesus did so with His disciples as He built faith into His men. He would test them by saying, *"O ye of little faith."* "Where is your faith?" He had to demonstrate His power to them time and time again. These periods of experiencing God in my life would sustain me through hard times and grievous trials. He would grant me grace to enlarge my faith to press on to higher altitudes with Him, where the air is more rarified and the view more exhilarating!

Allow me to give you a couple of instances in my life where God stepped in to build my faith and to make me into a man of faith. It was 2am and I felt like I was dying. At the time I was working sixteen hours a day, I would work eight hours at my secular job as a stockbroker, and eight hours with ministry work that God had called me to do. I was only getting three or four hours of sleep each night I would drop into bed after midnight and be up at 4:30 am to have my quiet time with God. Well, this particular night I felt like I was having a heart attack so I got up from bed and walked across the hall into my study and I plopped down at my desk before my open Bible. And I prayed to God to come get me and take me to heaven—I was so fatigued and worn out and ready to go be with Him in glory. Suddenly a presence was near me and He asked me a question (Jesus usually answered a question with a question in the Gospels), it was not an audible human voice but it was the VOICE. "What do you do for a living?"

"Investments," I replied.

"I have an investment in you and I will receive the dividends from my investment."

That's all I needed to hear. Case closed. I went back to bed. That was eighteen years ago, and I hope He has been receiving His dividends off my life like He said.

The second instance of Him building faith in me was when He showed up in revival at a church where I was preaching. I had not planned on preaching at all that week. I was on vacation and looking forward to playing some golf but it was a Wednesday afternoon and I telephoned a pastor I had just met a couple of months earlier to inform him I was in his town on vacation but I wanted to drop by his church for Wednesday service and worship. I called to get directions and the time of service for that evening. He gave me the information then he called me back twenty minutes later and asked me to take the Wednesday evening service and preach to his congregation. I had no sermon prepared. I had no suit with me. I was on vacation. And he wanted me to bring a message in less than four hours! I prayed about it and called him back and said I would be there. That evening the Lord led me to preach out of Amos chapter four regarding the subject of the Remedial Judgements of God. As I spoke to his people, I noticed many were weeping. When the service was over the pastor approached me and said,

> "When I preach the people leave talking and laughing. But when you preached their eyes were red and they left in complete silence."

It was obvious to me that God wanted to do a work in that church among His people. But I was on vacation and had no further ministry plans for that week. The pastor asked me to speak to his men on a Saturday morning at church at 10am. To bring them a message just for men. I showed up at 10 am that Saturday morning and spoke to about thirty men in a classroom. The pastor wanted me to speak for about forty five minutes to them. Seven hours later we were still at church in that room and God was at work among those men. There was much repentance and tears and praying and getting right with God.

I had to be back at my office on Monday morning and I had a flight out of town Sunday. But the pastor of the church called me Saturday night around 8 pm to ask me to take the Sunday morning service at his church the next day. I said I was due to fly out and go back home. He begged me to stay and preach. I said I would pray about it and call him back in an hour. I called a preacher friend of mine and told him what was going on and he said to cancel my flight and stay at that church because it was obvious God was at work. I called the pastor back and said I would preach for him in the morning. That night was spent out of bed on my knees, crying out to God in intercessory prayer for those people and that church and for God to move among them.

That Sunday morning I looked like a goof (this was back when preachers still wore a suit and tie to preach not blue jeans and casual wear!). I had no suit. I found an old out of style tie and wore that with a long sleeve shirt and my khaki golf pants. I had chosen for my text Revelation chapter twenty on the Great White Throne Judgment. I hit it hard and pressed man's duty of repentance on them as I preached about eternity and a God in that eternity. About half way through the sermon it looked as if a cannon ball had been shot down the center aisle of that church. The people looked alarmed. I finished and I said, "If there is anyone who wants to come down front for counseling and prayer do so and will the deacons now come forward to help with the counseling. No one moved an inch. I thought they had misunderstood me, so I repeated the request for the deacons to come down front and help with counseling. No one moved. It was dead silence. I closed my Bible and left the platform and took my seat on the front row. But I could not sit still. I fell to my knees and with my back to the congregation I raised my arms over my head and I was worshiping a holy God! I heard footsteps coming up the aisle for counseling. Then, suddenly a young man bounded up the aisle, jumping up and down, and hollering, "I just got saved! I just got saved! I really just got saved!"

Afterwards one of the deacons approached me and apologized and said, "We could not get up from our chair in answer to you—it was as if we were held frozen in our seats!"

And the music minister walked up to me with tears in his eyes and a smile on his face exclaiming, "I saw Jesus sitting on His Throne! I saw Jesus sitting on His Throne!"

I believe it could all be traced back to the day I asked God to make me a man of faith. What are you trusting God for friend? Where is your faith?

CHAPTER THREE

THE MAN GOD USES:
IS A MAN OF THE BIBLE

❖ "God's Word is true and God is true to His
Word"

E. A. Johnston

I was at a Bible conference where John Phillips, the Bible commentator, was speaking and he related a story pertinent to our subject regarding being a man of the Bible. He said he was with a Moody Bible Institute professor who was in his sixties and he had just finished giving a lecture on the Bible. A man from the audience approached him afterwards and shook his hand and thanked him for his talk and he remarked, "I sure wish I had your knowledge of the Bible!" And this professor looked at the man who was in his fifties and said to him: "Sir, you will NEVER have my knowledge of the Bible!" and with that he turned and walked away.

Well, he was a rude professor but he spoke the truth. What he was insinuating to this man was the fact that a man in his fifties who has not made the Bible his life work of study will not have the same knowledge of the Bible as a man who has devoted his lifetime to study it.

I came to Christ in a revival meeting as a thirteen-year-old boy and my first Bible was given to me in 1968 by a pastor who would not let me go to Hell. He was a neighbor, and he began praying for me to be saved—he saw that I was growing up in a godless home. He gave me my first job in his Bible bookstore when I was a teen. And he took an interest in my soul, and he presented me with two Bibles as gifts and he inscribed them to me. I still have those two Bibles today—they mean much to me. I developed a interest in the Bible at a young age. I went on to seminary to earn a doctorate in biblical studies, which further advanced my knowledge of the Bible. I was a Sunday school teacher for fifteen years and this too helped me develop my knowledge of the Bible as I had to prepare lessons each week. I also led a men's discipleship group in my home for years where I trained men in what I knew about God and the Bible and this too made me stay glued to my Bible. I eventually wrote a book, a Bible survey of each book of the Bible outlining the key word of each book, key chapter, main characters, theology and doctrines. God called me to preach and I have preached over two thousand sermons (see SermonAudio Evangelism Awakening) I am now sixty nine years old and have much of my life in the study of God's Word. I say all this to state a fact. The man God uses is a man of the Bible.

It is critically important to immerse yourself in the Word of God if you want to get to know the God of the Word and be more useful to Him. The problem today for many Christians is distractions from the world, career, family which intrude on the time normally spent on the study of God's Word. Sadly, there are some pastors who are more concerned about their golf handicap than their Bible knowledge so they spend little time in the Word of God—and it shows in their preaching! Men of former times lived in their Bibles and when they preached they made mention of it in all their illustrations—they knew their Bibles far better and more deeply than many of us today. When I was doing research on the underground church in China to prepare for a conference in Atlanta where I was to speak on the underground church, I learned that the average Chinese Christian in China has memorized much of their Bibles—in fact many are walking Bibles, able to quote entire books of the Bible! The scarcity of Bibles in China and the persecution of the church in China has made the Word of God precious to the Chinese Christians. We Americans take our Bibles for granted and seldom use them as we should.

If you are serious about being more useful to God with what is left of your life then you must become a student of the Bible. You must not only go through it completely but it must go completely through you! I have made use of some special Bibles through the years that have helped me grasp the Word of God more effectively. I will list them for you know friend and I hope you will go out and buy at least one of them and use it daily in your study of the Word of God.

I have found the following study Bibles to be a great resource to me through the years. In fact, I have worn out my original copies and had to replace all three of them! I will now list them for you and explain their usefulness. Which Bible translation you prefer is up to you. I prefer the King James Version. You can obtain these study Bibles in several translations.

1. *Key Word Study Bible*, also known as THE HEBREW-GREEK KEY WORD STUDY BIBLE by Spiros Zodhiates. This helpful tool has been immensely useful to me through the years as it provides the meaning of words in the original Hebrew and Greek language. It also has a Greek dictionary in the back.

2. *THOMPSON CHAIN REFERENCE BIBLE*. This helpful resource has an analytical and synthetic system of Bible study. This Bible will provide a chain of Bible subjects that you can trace all throughout the Scripture to see the Word of God in a more clear light. I cannot

emphasize enough the usefulness of this Bible study.

3. *MATTHEW HENRY STUDY BIBLE.* George Whitefield read the Bible commentary of the Puritan Matthew Henry on his knees as well as reading the Bible on his knees. I tried to read my Bible on my knees and gave up—I'm no Whitefield! This useful Bible Study will provide insight into Scripture via Matthew Henry's commentary which is priceless! I am always blessed by his spirit-led comments.

Regarding how I study my Bible I go through entire chapters in my daily quiet time. I refrain from the "lucky dip" and I have a system I use to study the Word of God. Every one of my Bibles is "marked up" with a pen, where I have left a date and time, and comments on how God had spoken to me on that particular day regarding the things I was going through in that particular time of my life. It has been useful for me to grab an old Bible and read what I wrote many years ago and ascertain my spiritual growth through the years. How you mark up your Bible is up to you, but I highly recommend that you do it. Here is a page from one of my Bibles:

A page from one of Dr. Johnston's Bibles

The man God uses is a man of the Bible. Be sure you devote more time to the study of the Word of God and you'll be glad you did!

CHAPTER FOUR

THE MAN GOD USES:
IS A MAN WHO WALKS WITH GOD

- ❖ "God is looking for a man that He can use to bless a nation and
- ❖ bring Him glory. The criteria are: availability, obedience, and
- ❖ faith."

E. A. Johnston

In the Book of Amos we read,

"Can two walk together, except they be agreed" (Amos 3:3)?

The answer is "no" they cannot. God is looking for a man He can use. Scripture teaches us that before God acts, He sends a man. He sent Moses to deliver a nation. He sent Elijah to turn a nation back to Him. He sent Jonah to save a nation for His glory. He sent His Son to suffer and die to reconcile a people back to Him.

In the Book of 1Kings we see how God builds a man into usefulness. God took Elijah and made him an instrument of revival that turned a nation back to God. We will look at the process that God took with His servant Elijah to discover how God builds a man He can use. Turn in your Bibles to 1Kings chapter seventeen where Elijah suddenly appears on the scene. In verse one we read:

> *"And Elijah the Tishbite who was of the inhabitants of Gilead, said unto Ahab, As the LORD God of Israel liveth, before whom I stand, there shall not be dew nor rain these years, but according to my word."*

God sent His prophet Elijah with a message for King Ahab, who was king of Israel. It is a message replete with a declaration, a judgment, and a warning. Ahab was a despot and a great sinner who provoked God Almighty with his grievous idol worship for we read in 1Kings 16:33,

> *"And Ahab made a grove; and Ahab did more to provoke the LORD God of Israel to anger than all the kings of Israel that were before him."*

And there was a long line of evil kings over Israel and Ahab was one of the worst! The prophet Elijah confronts this wicked king with a word from Jehovah God. Elijah makes the statement that *"his God lives"*; He is a living God as opposed to the dead dumb idols that Ahab was serving. The prophet makes mention of a remedial judgment to come as a result of all the idolatry and wickedness in the land, and that the remedial judgment will come in the form of a drought. And Elijah left Ahab standing there with his mouth open and fire in his eyes for his reproof. Ahab would eventually call Elijah "a troubler of Israel (1Kings 18:17).

We will now examine how God builds a man to walk with Him and to be used of Him. First God instructs Elijah to go hide himself by the brook Cherith. To go to a place of solitude to shut himself up with God in prayer. God promises His servant provision. And we see Elijah's obedience to God and his faith in God. This is all described here in verse three through six:

> *"Get thee hence, and turn thee eastward, and hide thyself by the brook Cherith, that is before Jordan. And it shall be, that thou shalt drink of the brook; and I have commanded the ravens to feed thee there. Elijah did according unto the word of the LORD: for he went and dwelt by the book Cherith that is before Jordan. And the ravens brought him bread and flesh in the morning, and bread and flesh in the evening, and he drank of the brook."*

God chose ravens as his food delivery for they could not carry but a few morsels in their small beaks. God told Elijah not to go to a feast but to be shut up to God in prayer. So here the first lesson in God's school is for His servant to learn his utter dependance upon God for all things. Each day's provision was only enough for that day. He had to trust God for tomorrow. God is building faith into Elijah, God is demonstrating His power over creation to Elijah. God is preparing Elijah for his confrontation on Mount Carmel with the prophets of Baal. And during this time of solitude by the brook Cherith, God is teaching His servant to trust in God and exercise his faith in God.

God then after a period of time (perhaps two years) God moves His servant away from the dried up brook as a result of the drought, to a place of provision in Zarephath a city in Zidon. There is a widow there whom God has commanded to sustain His prophet. But the ways of God are not the ways of man, she is not a wealthy widow with plenty of provision but a poor helpless widow almost out of provision herself! Here God teaches Elijah that *"with God all things are possible"*. Elijah finds her at the gate of the city gathering sticks for her last meal for she and her son. And Elijah asks her for a drink and some bread and she informs him of her desperate situation:

> *"And she said, As the LORD thy God liveth, I have not a cake, but an handful of meal in a barrel, and a little oil in a cruse: and, behold, I am*

> *gathering two sticks, that I may go in and dress it for me and my son, that we may eat it, and die"* (1Kings 17:12).

Elijah encourages her and declares God's provision for her and her son during these hard times,

> *"And Elijah said unto her, Fear not; go and do as thou hast said: but make me thereof a little cake first, and bring it unto me, and after make for thee and for thy son. For thus saith the LORD God of Israel, The barrel of meal shall not waste, neither shall the cruse of oil fail, until the day that the LORD sendeth rain upon the earth"* (1Kings 17:13,14).

We find from this striking passage of Scripture that God's Word is true and that God is true to His Word, for we read,

> *"And the barrel of meal wasted not, neither did the cruse of oil fail, according to the word of the LORD, which he spake by Elijah"* (v 16).

God is teaching Elijah faith. God is teaching Elijah how to walk in a close intimate walk with Him. Teaching His prophet that he can not only trust Him, he can experience Him and His power! God then increases Elijah's faith through the death and recovery of the widow's son. The widow's son dies and Elijah goes to God and cries out to God in prayer for the lad's life to be restored to him. And God performs yet another miracle through Elijah—this is the first instance in Scripture of the dead being raised to life! God is preparing Elijah for a mighty revival in the land that will begin atop Mount Carmel in a bitter contest between His God and the gods of Baal! But before Elijah departs from the widow's house, she makes a bold declaration about him:

"And the woman said to Elijah, Now by this I know that thou art a man of God, and that the word of the LORD in thy mouth is true" (v.24).

When God makes a man of God to walk with Him others will take notice!

We will now examine chapter eighteen of 1Kings and see how God uses a man to perform His work and bring Him glory! In this case a mighty revival which turns a people back to the God of the Bible!

Most of us are already familiar with the contest atop Mount Carmel between the prophets of Baal and God's man Elijah. The prophets of Baal outnumber Elijah. We see in the following verses of Scripture, where Elijah is telling King Ahab of the contest between the false gods and the true God:

"Now therefore send, and gather to me all Israel unto mount Carmel, and the prophets of Baal four hundred and fifty, and the prophets of the groves four hundred, which eat at Jezebel's table. Ahab sent unto all the children of Israel and gathered the prophets together unto mount Carmel" (1 Kings 18:19,20).

For the last three years God had been building His man for the task at hand. Whenever God is ready to act He SENDS A MAN. God is looking for such a man. His man.

"For the eyes of the LORD run to and fro throughout the whole earth, to show himself strong in the behalf of them whose heart is perfect toward him" (2 Chronicles 16:9).

Elijah addresses the assembled crowd atop Mount Carmel:

"And Elijah came unto all the people, and said, How long halt ye between two opinions? if the LORD be God, follow him: but if Baal, then follow him. And the people answered him not a word" (1 Kings 18:21).

Two main things were accomplished here atop Mount Carmel:

1. The people see with their own eyes that the god Baal they have been serving is a dead god who cannot hear or respond. For all the shouting and jumping and cutting with knives of the prophets of Baal could not get their god to respond and consume the sacrifice (1 Kings 18:22-29).

2. They witness the awesome power of the Living God who not only consumes the sacrifice but licks up all the water in the trenches (1 Kings 18: 30-38). We read in verses 37-39,

> *"Hear me, O LORD, hear me, that this people may know that thou art the LORD God, and that thou hast turned their heart back again. Then the fire of the LORD fell, and consumed the burnt sacrifice, and the wood, and the stones, and the dust, and licked up the water that was in the trench. And when all the people saw it, they fell on their faces: and they said, "The LORD, he is the God; the LORD, he is the God."*

God had called His servant Elijah, God had trained His servant Elijah, God had made His servant Elijah into a man of God who walked with God and whom God could depend on to be useful to Him for the good of His people and for His glory! And now God thrusts His servant Elijah onto the stage at the right time to turn a nation back to God in a glorious revival! We see this *"moving atop the mulberry trees"* this revival commences when Elijah declares to old rotten King Ahab,

> *"And Elijah said unto Ahab, Get thee up, eat and drink; for there is a sound of abundance of rain"* (v41).

But before the blessing can come, there is still work to do! Elijah the man of God must seek God in earnest, fervent prayer on the behalf of the land: we see in the following passage:

> *"So Ahab went up to eat and to drink. And Elijah went up to the top of Carmel; and he cast himself down upon the earth, and put his face between his knees. And said to his servant, Go up now, look toward the sea. And he went up, and look, and said, There is nothing. And he said, Go again seven times. And it came to pass at the seventh time, that he said, Behold, there ariseth a little cloud out of the sea, like a man's hand. And he said, Go up, say unto Ahab, Prepare thy chariot, and get thee down, that the rain stop thee not. And it came to pass in the meanwhile, that the heaven was black with clouds and wind, and there was a great rain. And Ahab rode, and went to Jezreel. And*

the hand of the LORD was on Elijah; and he girded up his loins, and ran before Ahab to the entrance of Jezreel" (1 Kings 18:42-46).

Revival had come! The people turned back to God! Heaven gave forth rain! And God had built a man He could use for His purpose and for His glory! The best description of the man God uses is found in the words, *"And the hand of the LORD was on Elijah"* (v. 46). The man God uses is a man who walks with God.

CHAPTER FIVE:
THE MAN GOD USES IS: AN EMPTY AND CLEAR CHANNEL

- ❖ "Be willing to be reduced to nothing, so He can be everything
- ❖ through you."

E. A. Johnston

God uses those servants of His who are empty of themselves and who are clear channels that He can flow through as a means of blessings to others. God builds His servants through His Divine Process of reducing and decreasing. Gold must be reduced to its purity in the furnace of affliction. A branch must be pruned back and decreased with a sharp knife before it can grow more fruit. If we desire further usefulness to God, then we must submit both to the Refiner's fire and the Divine Pruning knife.

John Sung, the Chinese evangelist was a man of God whom God used to bring a mighty revival to China during the mid 20th century, just before World War II. John Sung's own personal story is a miracle in itself. Born in China and educated in America, he earned a Ph.D. in chemistry and spoke four languages fluently. He was a genius who had offers from high profile Universities all over the world to come be their professor. Instead, he chose to go to seminary at Union Bible College in New York City. It was there that he lost his faith under the liberal teaching of staff. But one evening in his dorm room in 1927, Jesus Christ visited him and he was radically saved similar to the Apostle Paul's conversion. Jesus changed his Chinese name to "John" and revealed to him that he would have a vital evangelistic ministry that would last fifteen years and shake China for God. These fifteen years were fit into a predetermined plan God had for John Sung (Eph. 2:10) and were to be separated by five three-year periods called: WATER, DOOR, DOVE, BLOOD, and TOMB.

John Sung's conversion experience was so radical that it completely changed his outward behavior. He would sing walking down the halls of the seminary while jumping up and down, and this alarmed his unregenerate professors who had him committed to a mental institution for 193 days. It was during this time that John Sung read his Bible forty four times! Getting a key word for each chapter which he would later use in ministry once he returned to China.

The WATER PERIOD began in 1927, and typified by water was to be a preparatory time and it commenced when he returned to China from America. The second period was the DOOR period from November 1930 to November 1933. And it was this time in John Sung's ministry that God began to open doors for him to preach and where God began to send revivals that attended Sung's preaching. The third period was the DOVE PERIOD, November 1933 to November 1936, and it was during this time that the Holy Spirit was poured out on the church in China. During this time Sung had asked God to give him 100,000 souls and God answered that prayer! He then asked God to give him 200,000 souls and God brought that harvest in as well. John Sung had a apostolic ministry of signs and wonders and many in his meetings were healed of disease and their limbs or sight were restored. Miracles attended his powerful ministry.

The fourth, or BLOOD PERIOD began November 1936 to 1939. And it was during this time that John Sung bled from inoperable hemorrhoids— he had to change his underwear after every time he preached and was in constant pain and suffering. His condition worsened to where he had to preach lying down. The fifth, or TOMB PERIOD occurred when he was shut up in the hospital as an invalid or secluded in his home in Peking. John Sung died at the age of 42. He is quoted as saying,

"I have made up my mind: even if I have to die, I will preach the Gospel in China. I will die a willing death, if only my fellowmen be saved!"[1]

I mention this ministry of John Sung to emphasize the man God uses. John Sung taught that a believer must become an "empty and clean" channel where the Holy Spirit can flow His Living Waters through to the blessings of others. He even had a sermon entitled, "Empty of Self". John Sung was a man of God surrendered to the discipline of the Spirit of God! The British evangelist and Bible teacher, J. Sidlow Baxter used to say, "How can a man full of himself preach the Christ who emptied Himself?"

John Sung was once asked by a fellow minister, "Why are your sermons so powerful?" Sung, replied, "because of my constant repentance." John Sung would preach all day and would spend most of the night out of bed and on his face before God in prayer. This is how he maintained a vital intimate walk with God and subsequently was an empty and clear channel that God could flow through as a means of revival and blessing to others! The man God uses is an empty and clear channel.

---

[1] Diary of John Sung by Levi his daughter. (Singapore: Genesis Books, 2008). Also, the pamphlet, "I Remember John Sung" by William Schubert.

CHAPTER SIX

THE MAN GOD USES: IS FULL OF THE HOLY GHOST

❖ "If Jesus told His men to tarry in the city until they

❖ were endued with power from on high, then we

❖ should do the same. We should not move one

❖ skinny inch for God without the power of God upon us."

E. A. Johnston

In the Book of Acts we read the words of Jesus, "But ye shall receive power, after that the Holy Ghost is come upon you: and ye shall be witnesses unto me both in Jerusalem, and in all Judea, and in Samaria, and unto the uttermost part of the earth" (Acts 1:8).

When I was taking my oral exam for my Ph.D. before two of my seminary professors, I said to one of them, "When I look at the Book of Acts and see how the early church had a power we do not have today and a vital Christianity we do not have today and I ask myself why? Why can't we have that?" And the seminary professor replied, "that was for that time. Not now."

And I was sitting in a preaching class and one of the students next to me raised his hand and asked the preaching professor the following question: he said, "When I study the history of revival and is see men like Jonathan Edwards full of the Holy Ghost and power with an anointing on his preaching, why can't we have that today?" And the seminary professor answered with a look of disdain and a voice of contempt, "You young man, are no Jonathan Edwards."

Unfortunately, they don't teach you how to preach in seminary—I know for I've graduated from two different seminaries with earned doctorates. Both of those egg-headed professors that threw cold water on me and my fellow student are living a mediocre Christian life void of any power from above. But that same power that was upon the early church is readily available for us today! John the Baptist spoke of such power, "John answered, saying unto them all, I indeed baptize you with water; but one mightier than I cometh, the latchet of whose shoes I am not worthy to unloose: he shall baptize you with the Holy Ghost and with fire" (Luke 3:16).

I have known men, men of God, who were baptized with this Holy Ghost power and who preached with that "fire." When they preached an anointing attended their ministry. My pastor Dr.

Adrian Rogers and my homiletical mentor, Dr. Stephen Olford were both men full of the Holy Ghost. I was sitting with Adrian Rogers in his study one day and I asked him when he felt he had received a special anointing from God. He got a faraway look in his eye and he replied, "It was right after my baby son died. Through my grief I went deeper with God then and He met me."

Let me share a story with you about my homiletical mentor, Dr. Stephen F. Olford. He was invited to go preach at a big Baptist church in Dallas, Texas and the pastor of that church asked his seminary intern to go to the airport to pick up Stephen Olford. "How will I recognize him? Do You have a photo of him?" the young man asked. "No need for that," replied the pastor, "just go to the airport terminal and wait for the passengers to deplane and look for a man who has "God all over him." Sure enough, when the young man went to the airport he watched a line of passengers walking toward him and there was a man with his coat over his arm and a briefcase in his hand and "he had God all over him." Like the Shunemite woman commented to her husband concerning Elisha the prophet,

> *"And she said to her husband, Behold now, I perceive that this is a holy man of God, which passeth by us continually"* (2 Kings 4:9).

Both Adrian Rogers and Stephen Olford shared a common denominator that is lacking in most ministers today: they were holy men of God. Holiness was a pursuit for them. In fact, Stephen Olford kept a framed copy of in his study of the quote of Robert Murray McCheyne, "Lord, make me as holy as a saved sinner can be!"

I can personally say that I have sat under the preaching of both Adrian Rogers and Stephen Olford for a number of years and they have this Holy Ghost power. Paul speaks of this in Romans,

> *"For I am not ashamed of the gospel of Christ: for it is the power of God unto salvation to every one that believeth; to the Jew first, and also to the Greek"* (Romans 1:16).

Evan Roberts, the man of God used so mightily during the Welsh Revival of 1904 (where it was said 100,000 souls were converted during that revival), was a man full of the Holy Ghost who was well familiar with "this fire". The last poem he wrote stated:

> Here I have built my altar,
>
> The wood I've placed in order;
>
> The sacrifice is ready now,
>
> Send thou, O Lord, the Fire.

My soul is weary, weak, and lustful,

But to the end I will be faithful;

Though hellish hosts revile forever,

I'll lay myself on Christ, my Savior.

Evan Roberts

Unfortunately, not everyone is a student of revival (and that includes most ministers). We must study men of God in former times whom God used in remarkable ways, especially in times of revival and spiritual awakening. I want to mention three men to you now whom God used and all three of these evangelists had a "second blessing" or this power from on high that attended their life and ministry. These three men are: Charles Finney, D. L. Moody, and Sam Jones. listen to their following stories of receiving "power from on high".

THE SECRET

It is no coincidence that the three most-used American evangelists of the 19th century each shared a common experience—an enduement of Holy Ghost power for service. It happened to Charles Finney, D. L. Moody and Sam Jones. this was the secret to their power. And this anointing occurred to each of them BEFORE they were thrust onto a national stage of great usefulness.

It came to Dwight Lyman Moody in 1871, before he was greatly used of God in revival throughout Great Britain. It happened to Charles Grandison Finney before he was used of God in revivals during the Second Great Awakening. And it happened to Samuel Porter Jones before he was thrust into the national spotlight and so powerfully used in revivals throughout the whole of America. We will examine these men one by one and compare their unique yet common experience,

In 1871 D. L. Moody was hungering for something more for God.

"An intense hunger and thirst for spiritual power was aroused in him by two women who

used to attend the meetings and sit in the front seat. He could see by the expression on

their faces that they were praying. At the close of the service they would say to him:

"'We have been praying for you.'

"'Why don't you pray for the people?' Mr. Moody would ask.

"'Because you need the power of the Spirit,' they would say...

"There came a great hunger in my soul. I did not know what it was. I began to cry out as

I never did before. I really felt that I did not want to live if I could not have this power

for service."[2]

D. L. Moody would speak of his experience of 1871 in future sermons and considered it the watermark highlight of his effectiveness for Christ and the gospel. Even near the end of his life in his last campaigns he would make mention of it.

"I was crying all the time that God would fill me with His Spirit. Well, one day, in the city

of New York—oh, what a day!—I cannot describe it. I seldom refer to it; it is almost too

sacred an experience to name. Paul had an experience of which he never spoke for

fourteen years. I can only say that God revealed Himself to me, and I had such an

experience of His love that I had to ask Him to stay His hand. I went to preaching again.

The sermons were no different; I did not present any new truths, and yet hundreds were

converted. I would not now be placed back where I was before that blessed experience

---

[2] William R. Moody, "The Life of Dwight L. Moody" (Chicago: Fleming Revell, 1900), pp 146-147.

if you should give me all the world—it would be as the small dust in the balance."[3]

Charles Finney had an identical experience of that of D. L. Moody, as we see from his Memoirs; he was newly converted and alone in his law office when the following incident occurred in 1821:

"But as I returned and was about to take a seat by the fire, I received a mighty

baptism of the Holy Ghost...the Holy Spirit descended upon me in a manner that

seemed to go through me, body and soul. I could feel the impression, like a wave of

electricity, going through and through me. Indeed it seemed to come in waves, and

waves of liquid love;--for I could not express it in any other way...these waves came

over me, and over me, and over me one after the other, until I recollect I cried out,

'I shall die if these waves continue to pass over me.' I said to the Lord, 'Lord, I cannot

bear anymore.'"[4]

---

[3] Ibid, p 149.

[4] A. G. Dupuis and Garth M. Rosell, "Memoirs of Charles Finney" (Grand Rapids: Academie Books, 1989), pp 23-24.

Samuel Porter Jones, before God used him in a larger capacity of national prominence and city wide revivals, he received the same anointing of Holy Ghost power as did Finney and Moody. Sam Jones was holding meetings in Corinth, Mississippi, in 1884 (prior to his being thrust into national prominence), when the following incident occurred:

"One of the most thrilling experiences of his life occurred there. he had become so

wearied and tired from constant preaching that one night going to church he said,

'I am so tired I cannot stand up and preach this evening. I shall ask the people if they

will allow me to sit down and talk to them.'

'Upon announcing his text, the baptism of the Holy Spirit came upon him, and when

he had finished the sermon, and had concluded a long altar service, he went away

from the church saying, 'I feel as if I were the best rested man on earth.' That night

in his room the Holy Spirit continued to bless him, until he cried out, "This is glorious,

the breezes of heaven are sweeping in upon my soul!' For ten minutes or more these waves of blessing passed over his spirit, and for three months or more he didn't

know the sense of fatigue as he labored day and night for the salvation of the lost."[5]

Immediately after Sam Jones received this baptism of Holy Ghost fire an entire town would be brought to Christ in the town of Tuscumbia, Alabama.

In 1874, in the town of Tuscumbia, Alabama, a F4 tornado ravaged the town, destroying a third of it and killing fourteen people. Ten years later in 1884, Samuel Porter Jones was in the town preaching four times a day in a God shaking revival that turned the little Alabama town upside down. We see from the following account that Sam Jones was a man of prayer whose sole reliance for power was the Holy Spirit: we say this to emphasize the fact that there was nothing special about Sam Jones the man, in the salvation of souls but in the Spirit of God who worked through the human instrument Sam Jones—all the glory goes to God in the salvation of souls. Salvation is of the Lord.

- "At Tuscumbia, Ala., he held a large bush-arbor meeting. Three and four services were

---

[5] Laura Jones, "Life and Sayings of Sam P. Jones"(Atlanta: The Franklin Turner Company, 1907), pp 113-114.

- held daily, and people came in from all parts of the country. Some of the most
- remarkable manifestations of the presence of God were seen in that arbor meeting.
- The people marveled at the results, and perhaps the secret was not known to them;
- however, it can be attributed to the earnest prayers of Mr. Jones. The great audiences
- that he preached to did not know how many times he wrestled with God in prayer
- before preaching. Just before the greatest manifestation of the Spirit's work, Mr. Jones
- had been very earnest in prayer. He was always a man who went to the throne of mercy
- for the anointing of service...there was a great crises in the meeting, and he met it by a
- long season of prayer.
- "The people had made all kinds of threats against him, so after the night service he
- walked out onto the second-story of the porch and knelt down in a corner, the thick
- vines almost hiding him. He remained there until midnight, and yet no assurance of
- victory. The morning hours came, and he was still on his knees. He had not undressed
- or been asleep that night. The great audience assembled for the six o'clock service;

- perhaps there were twenty-five hundred present. He arose to preach, and such power
- came upon the people that the town was won to God.[6]
- One thing is certain: the man God uses is a man full of the Holy Ghost!

---

[6] E. A. Johnston, "Sam Jones A New Biography" (Georgia: The Old Paths Publications, 2023), pp 188-191.

CHAPTER SEVEN

THE MAN GOD USES IS: ABLE TO TEACH OTHERS

> ❖ "I was discipled by two Christian men who inspired me
> ❖ to have my own discipleship group for men which met in
> ❖ my home for years."
>
> E. A. Johnston

I was discipled by two Christian men and they inspired me to have my own discipleship group in my home for years. It met every Tuesday evening at 7:00pm and Friday morning at 6:00am. We read of the Apostle Paul's exhortation to his disciple Timothy,

> *"And the things that thou hast heard of me among many witnesses, the same commit thou to faithful men, who shall be able to teach others"* (2 Timothy 2:2).

The Apostle Paul had Timothy and Titus to pour his life into as his disciples. The man God uses is a trainer of men. What are you doing with your leisure time friend? Watching tv or playing sports or enjoying a hobby? Why not dust off your Bible and pray for God to send you a man to disciple (or if you are a woman a woman to disciple). God gets serious with those who get serious with Him. After I was discipled by those other two men I prayed to God to bring some men to me, and I promised Him if He did I would sacrifice the time to disciple them. After that prayer I had fourteen men sitting in a circle in my living room! I spent decades discipling men. I even wrote a book on discipleship entitled, "No Turning Back" (published by Gospel Folio Press).

Jesus, when He was here in His earthly ministry was not concerned with numbers like we are. We like to brag if we have 3,000 on Sunday in our church—but most of the time He had twelve. He spent most of His time pouring His life into those twelve men. My friend, the late Bible commentator, William MacDonald (who wrote *"The Believer's Bible Commentary"*, and *"True Discipleship"*) made a statement that has always stuck with me. Bill MacDonald wrote:

> "We often think that it must have been a wonderful experience to travel with Jesus when He was here on earth. We can see Him and His disciples sauntering along, enjoying a continual Bible conference. But it wasn't like that. It was more of a scalding experience in which the disciples learned their own sinfulness and

failure, and in which they were called to a pathway of persecution, suffering, and death."

A discipleship group can be one of the most rewarding blessings of a ministry. I have seen men's lives transformed to the very glory of God! I have seen God move in revival in a group of men and change their homelife! I have seen businessmen who would never dream of going to the foreign field with the Gospel, get on fire for souls and take several short-term mission trips to such destinations as Africa, Central America, and South America. We should each be disciple makers for the Great Commission is an exhortation to all followers of Jesus *"to go and make disciples"*:

> *"And Jesus came and spake unto them saying, All power is given unto me in heaven and in earth. Go ye therefore, and teach all nations, baptizing them in the name of the Father, and of the Son, and the Holy Ghost: teaching them to observe all things whatsoever I have commanded you: and, lo, I am with you always, even to the end of the world"* (Matthew 28:18-20).

Perhaps you may wish to pray for a person or persons to disciple. A word to the wise, keep it men discipling men, and women discipling women to avoid any questions of discretion.

Also, try to keep the group comprised of individuals who are in agreement with the doctrine of your denomination. This is very important. Unhappy is the man who starts a group full of Methodists, Presbyterians, Southern Baptists, Independent Baptists, and Church of Christ or any others. The heated arguments over doctrine will divide the group; differing beliefs over Calvinism, Arminianism, Baptism, salvation and so on will ruin the meetings. I was discipled by two other men and my first discipleship group where I was the learner, it was comprised of 99% Southern Baptists except for a hard-boiled Calvinist. The Calvinist ended up reforming one of the Baptists and he left the church! So keep it on a level playing field denominationally and theologically from the beginning. Only allow those whom you invited to participate, be wary of the uninvited visitor! Usually, this person is disruptive to the entire group. A friend-of-a-friend needs to be discipled by that friend, not you.

I have a tried and tested format that I used for my own discipleship group and it worked well for several decades. I will share it with you and perhaps you can use it in your own group (with some modifications).

Here is my discipleship format:

There must be a predetermined format for the group. This keeps it interesting and organized. Bear in mind you must make allowances for the Holy Spirit to move. However, a set format is helpful, useful and impacting. And impact is the key word! A disciple means "learner", so you are teaching others what you have learned in your Christian walk. The goal of disciple making is to "move men." To effect change. This is what Jesus did with His disciples. He took a group of unlearned, men and instructed them with His teachings to make them better men, more useful men for the kingdom of God and the Father's glory! We must follow Christ's example here. He called men to Himself, then He transformed them into new men. Old wine could no longer be placed into new wineskins! This is critically important to disciple making. Otherwise, you run the risk of your group becoming "just another Bible study or fellowship group." Just because you have some people meeting at your house once a week and chatting and having a "good time" does not mean you have a discipleship group! Please keep this in mind. The purpose of the group or one-on-one meetings is to teach and transform individuals to impact the world for Christ and the Gospel!

FORMAT

First, choose a set day once a week. Then pick the place to meet. Then determine the time of the meeting. Decide if you want to serve refreshments or coffee. My first group (which consisted of fourteen men) met at my home on Tuesday evenings from 7pm to 8:30pm. This worked well because most of the men had already eaten dinner and had already been with their family a little while before driving to my house. This gave them time to "put-off" the business of the day and re-focus on spiritual things. I have had smaller groups or even one-on-one meetings meet at my home on Friday mornings at 6am to 7am (this gave them ample time to get to work). It is a commitment to be at someone's house at 6am! what counts costs and what costs counts! And being a disciple is all about commitment and surrender.

WHAT TO STUDY

It is important that you know where you are going with your group or individual. Do not make this time just a Bible study and fellowship—that is not what true discipleship is all about. It is about training. You are training individuals to be more effective leaders and witnesses for Jesus Christ. Pray that the Lord would show you what direction to take with this particular group or individual. His purposes are best and listening to the guidance of the Holy Spirit is the right way to begin any discipleship training program.

Before I began my first group I went to hear Henry Blackaby preach at a local church in my community. I made it a point to get some one-on-one time with him to get his advice on this matter. I asked him, "I am starting a discipleship group. What advice can you give me as to what I should teach them?" Dr. Blackaby paused, prayed with his eyes closed and then answered: "Jesus had some specific truths to teach His men and He taught those truths to them until they got them." That was good advice.

Here are some suggestions I have used which you may find helpful:

One: Reading Material: Books that I recommend for spiritual growth and personal revival are: Christian biographies—we learn much from the study of men and women God has used in former times. Biographies on men like George Whitefield, Charles Finney, D. L. Moody, Sam Jones and Mordecai Ham can be very worthwhile and helpful. I highly recommend David Brainerd's Journal and John Sung's Journal.

Two: Books on Discipleship: "True Discipleship" by William MacDonald is very helpful. Bill was a personal friend and his book sold over one million copies! He never took a dime from the profits and put all proceeds into foreign translation of his bible commentary "Believers Bible Commentary." Bill MacDonald lived very frugally and gave all to Christ and the Gospel. His desk in his spartan apartment in San Leandro, California was a door took off its hinges and placed atop two chairs! Bill was a life-long disciple maker.

Three: Map of the world or a big globe. I would use a map of the world or a big globe with my group to get them focused on foreign countries. Each week we would pray for a particular country for the spread of the Gospel and salvation. I would suggest you obtain a copy of "Operation World" by Patrick Johnstone and use it with your map or globe to pray over the nations highlighted in the book. Each county is listed with its geography, population, spiritual needs and growth, as well as number of missionaries there. This will keep your disciples focused on the world for God is a global God!

Four: Books on Prayer: Prayer is the oil that moves the wheels of God's activity in the world. Reading good books on prayer is highly useful for your own prayer life as well as that of your group. I highly recommend books on prayer by E. M. Bounds, Samuel Chadwick, or other men God has used in former times. "Rees Howells Intercessor" by Norman Grubb, is a must-have for any serious student of prayer.

Five: Books on Holiness and Christian living: "Born Crucified" by L. E. Maxwell; "Bone of my Bone" by F. J. Huegal; "The Christ Life for the Self Life" by F. B. Myer; "Absolute Surrender" by Andrew Murray; "Not I But Christ" by Stephen Olford.

Six: Books on Revival: I cannot emphasize this enough! Please read as many books about revival as you possibly can. I have studied revival for over four decades and have read and re-read hundreds of books on revival through the years. If you want to see God move in our day in revival, then you must study how God has moved in former times among His people. Books on revival are critically important to any serious believer. Some suggestions are:

"Revival" by Martyn Lloyd-Jones.

"Fire In The Church" by Ted Rendell.

"Heart Cry For Revival" by Stephen Olford.

"Revival" by Richard Owen Roberts

"Revival Trilogy" by E. A. Johnston.

Seven: Bible Commentaries: this list is endless and personal preference will narrow the field. Matthew Henry's *Bible Commentary* will be very useful to you.

Eight: Read your Bible! Immerse yourself in God's Word until it goes right through you! Become a student of the Bible. I have been studying the Bible since 1968. I went to seminary to get a doctorate in Biblical Studies. I still pour over my Bible every day! God's Word must become a reality in your life.

WHAT TO TEACH

Teaching your disciples is what disciple making is all about! As you train them with what you have learned as a believer and help them to experience personal revival themselves, then you have pointed them in the right direction for going deeper with God. Remember, first change the man; then change his vision. The main goal is to get others into a white hot love relationship with Jesus that grows on a daily basis through the pursuit of God. God's Word is true and He is true to His Word. Remember, *"that he is a rewarder of them that diligently seek Him"* (Hebrews 11:6).

Next, it is time to change their vision. *"Where there is no vision, the people perish"* (Proverbs 29:18). You must get them to see "the world" through the lens of God's eyes from His perspective. Your disciples must "catch the vision" of reaching the world for Christ and fulfilling His mandate in the Great Commission. Your goal is to build a world-visionary, world-impacting, reproducing disciple who will go and train others. This is the multiplication effect! Regarding your group of men, you will be able to tell early on who is there just for fellowship and soaking and those who are on fire for God and the spread of the Gospel. Spend more one-on-one time with the "go-getters". Paul poured his life into his disciples, Timothy and Titus, and they in turn trained other faithful men. This is true disciple reproduction that glories God and is biblical!

Do not underestimate the power of compounding interest: Your disciples, if trained properly, go out "and do likewise". Here is an illustration: If I give you one penny on the first day of the month and offer to double the sum each day for thirty-one days, or offer you a cool million dollars, which offer would you take? Taking the cool million would cost you almost ten million dollars! Where did it start? With one penny! So it is with your disciples, if you get the right men (or woman if you get the right women) and train them properly you will have a vast multiplication effect!

THE HOUR MEETING

Most discipleship meetings should last one hour. Some can go ninety minutes but that is stretching it! Keep it to an hour and the time will pass quickly and it will keep your group hungry for more next time. From time to time it is good to play a DVD of a godly saint to inspire the group. I have had great success with an interview of Leonard Ravenhill right before he died. I have also played audio sermons of Duncan Campbell's testimony and the revival on the Isle of Lewis in Scotland. Anything you can add to enhance and inspire your group will be useful.

When I was hosting my weekly Tuesday evening meeting my wife would prepare a food tray with snacks on it and fresh lemonade for the men to grab after the meeting and have a little fellowship time. I would have a basket with Scripture verses on them to memorize for the week and we would pass the basket around and the following week I would have each man repeat his verse from memory—this brought out their competitive nature so not to look bad in front of the other men by not bothering to memorize the verse. I had a coffee table stacked with books that I bought for my men: these were paperback biographies of the "Men of Faith" series by Penguin Books. I encouraged them to grab a book and when finished with it, grab another one to learn about these "Men of Faith" whom God had used. Men like Charles Spurgeon, D. L. Moody, Charles Finney, John Wesley, and other lesser-known men who were men of faith like: Borden of Yale, and Samuel Morris. The point was to get my men familiar with spiritual giants whom God had used in former times so that it would inspire them. One anecdotal story: when I was at work one day a man from my discipleship group dropped by my house and asked my wife if he could borrow the stack of

"Men of Faith" books on the table and he cleaned me out and never returned them and I never saw him again!

The following format is what I used for my Friday morning group which met at my house at 6am.

1) I greet them. There is a pot of hot coffee and some breakfast bars awaiting them. I allow five minutes for them to greet one another.

2) We begin with prayer. The last group I discipled had five hand-picked men who were deeply committed to growing in Christ and actively pursuing Him! I ask one man to begin in prayer and we go around the room. They know not to be long-winded, they pray short prayers. Then I close in prayer, asking the Lord to bless the meeting.

3) Then I open my Bible and share with the men a portion of God's Word from which the Lord has spoken to me this week and geared for the discipleship group. It is amazing how faithful God is in helping me lead the group by giving me vital insights into the Scripture study for that day.

4) Next, I lead the men in the area of discussion regarding their needs this week and upcoming month. Health needs, work-related needs, spiritual needs, domestic needs. This is where

the men unburden their hearts and are transparent.

5) Then I ask if there are any prayer requests that we need to be aware of or any mission trips coming up in which we need to pray about. In my last group I had two men who were going on short-term mission trips with the church and we would pray for those needs (financial and spiritual). As these men learn to pray for one another it binds the group together. Those who do not go on the mission trips "hold the ropes" for the ones that do. There is a special bond realized between the men. This is a very important aspect to the group! Jesus did not spend most of His time in front of vast crowds preaching. He spent most of His time with His men training them to go reach the masses!

6) I pray for the men. I pray for their families. I pray for their walk in Christ and for protection for each of them from the Enemy. I pray for Jesus to undergird them as they go out for this day.

7) We then break for refreshments and good-byes until next week! Often I would receive phone calls from the men during the week with prayer requests or issues they are facing. If one was in a crises I would make time to meet him for lunch and counsel him one-on-one. Being a disciple maker is a 24/7 task! I

have been called out of bed after midnight to rush to a man's home because of a distressed call from a worried wife because her husband needed someone to pray for him right then! As a discipler of men, one must be willing to always go "the extra mile" on the road of discipleship. It pays wonderful dividends that last for eternity!

IN CLOSING: allow me to make a few more suggestions. There will always come a day when it is time for you to "close your present group down". In other words, you cannot and should not disciple someone indefinitely. All the while you are training someone, always keep reminding them that you are training them so they can go out and train others! There is a Graduation Day. This is critically important. If you fail to effectively communicate this, the "doubling of pennies" stops and mass reproduction loses effectiveness. You are "pouring your life" into them so "they can go out and do the same for someone else." They must understand this concept throughout the entire process. Tell the at the beginning, that the end game for them is to go out and train someone else what they have learned from you. this is the "2 Timothy Principle" (2 Timothy 2:2). Make them memorize that text! The man God uses is a man who teaches others. Go and get your man!

CHAPTER EIGHT

THE MAN GOD USES IS:
A SEARCHING PREACHER

- ❖ "We need God-called preachers anointed with the Holy Ghost who
- ❖ preach "searching sermons" with the force of a volcano, where
- ❖ every word falls with the weight of a hammer; burns like a fire;
- ❖ and cuts like a knife."

E. A. Johnston

We read in the Book of Amos:

"Behold, the days come, saith the LORD God, that I will send a famine in the land, not a famine of bread, nor a thirst for water, but of hearing the words of the LORD" (Amos 8:11).

One would be hard pressed to find a real God-called preacher in the land today. They exist, but they are in dwindling numbers as the older God-called preachers are replaced with CEO's or teachers. Teachers inform, preachers transform. This is why there is so little spiritual transformation occurring in our churches today—most of the ministers are teachers and not preachers.

Unfortunately, many men in ministry view the size of their campus and numerical membership as success in ministry. If you are running 3,000 on Sunday all is well. But the true success of any ministry is the impact made on eternity! Success is not measured by brick and mortar and numbers but by lives transformed by the Spirit of God! And many churches today hire pastors based on their ability to run an organization and to grow it numerically; but not to develop spiritual growth in the lives of its members.

I will share with you an interesting true story. Years ago, I was asked to do a radio interview on Christian radio and the female moderator related the following story to me.

She said that she once had a job that was eye opening in regard to ministry. She said she was hired by an organization to conduct a religious poll on the ministry and her job was to randomly telephone pastors around the country and ask them the following question: "Why did you become a pastor?" She told me that she contacted 1,000 ministers all across America and she was shocked by their answers to why they entered the ministry. She related that one man said he became a pastor because he was a single man and he wanted to meet women! Another man said, that he was gifted with a winning personality that attracted crowds so that is why he became a pastor. Another man said, he wanted to be a help to the downtrodden in his community, so he thought the best way to do that was to become a pastor of a church. One man interviewed said he was a good public speaker so this occupation best fit his talent. Another man said he had graduated seminary and earned a doctor degree and so this was the reason for becoming a minister, because he was properly educated.

This radio host told me that after speaking to hundreds and hundreds of ministers across the country they each had a reason to become a minister and it was mostly self-motivated. Out of the 1,000 men contacted, only one man, she told me, had a different answer from all the rest. He was a black pastor in the South and he said the main reason he became a pastor was because God called him. The greatest need in our nation today is God-called preachers! This is our only hope for revival!

Personally, I was at a pastor's conference years ago and I asked the man seated next to me why he became a pastor. This is what he told me: he said, "I was a High School Math teacher but I got fired. I then went to work for an accounting firm but that didn't work out too well. Then I tried opening my own business but it failed to take off. So, I thought I'd try being a pastor, that's why I am at this conference." Pity the poor congregation that gets this failure as a pastor! We need God-called men full of the Holy Ghost to stand in our pulpits once again!

But our desperate need is not just for a God-called preacher, but one who preaches searching sermons. Preaching that awakens sinners to their lost condition and brings Holy Ghost conviction. A preacher who knows how to preach the law before grace and bring a sinner to Mt. Sinai that is "altogether on a smoke" and confront him with the strictness and severity of God's holy law, and then point him to Calvary and Mt. Zion!

The Church is in a sad spiritual declension and many of our denominations are fallen into apostacy. Society grows more evil every day and it is as if a moral sewar has spilled out upon this nation with sin and perversion! Where is the God-called man who will preach the full counsel of God and proclaim the great doctrines of the Gospel? Which are Ruin, Redemption, Repentance, and Regeneration! Like Adrian Rogers said: "We need God-called men to pick up the Book of God and preach it with an anointing of the Spirit of God."

I was at the funeral of my homiletical mentor, Dr. Stephen F. Olford, and Dr. Adrian Rogers was conducting the service. Afterwards, in the hallway of Bellevue Baptist in Memphis, Dr. Rogers and I were talking, as he was my friend and pastor. He was standing with his arms folded across his chest and he had a stern look on his face and he said: "Do you know what concerns me?"

I said, "No, Dr. Rogers. What concerns you?"

He said, "I see God calling up men like Stephen Olford and Sidlow Baxter, and I look around and I don't see any "come-uppers!" And he knew everybody!

What we need today are some "come-uppers" to come and preach the Old God-centered Gospel! We will now examine what the true Gospel is and how to preach it in an impacting way to bring souls to Christ for salvation. Unfortunately, the rise of the "Easy Believe Gospel" has done much damage to modern evangelism and produced many spurious conversions. We must ask ourselves a question: is a man saved by a decision he makes? Or by a supernatural work of grace performed by the Spirit of God in regeneration?

Jesus taught that salvation was found along a narrow way and few there were to find it. And evangelists took up the bandwagon of an Easy Believe Gospel and broadened the way of salvation in ways Jesus never did. Jesus said:

> *"Enter ye in at the strait gate: for wide*
> *is the gate, and broad is the way, that*

leadeth to destruction, and many there be which go in thereat: because strait is the gage, and narrow is the way, which leadeth unto life, and few there be that find it" (Matthew 7:13-14).

Then, remarkably Jesus in the next sentence warns His followers of false prophets, "Beware of false prophets, which come to you in sheep clothing (or a seminary professor's chair), but inwardly they are ravening wolves" (Matthew 7:15).

There is an urgent need to preach a true biblical Gospel. It has been estimated that 83 people a minute on the globe die without Christ. Do the math, that is almost 5,000 an hour. That is 120,000 a day! That adds up to roughly one million souls weekly dropping into a Devil's Hell! That comes to almost 4,000,000 people perishing a month into the regions of darkness and misery! Keep doing the math and you will find that it adds up to approximately 40 million souls being swept away down to a Devil's Hell to suffer for all eternity! Go back to the beginning of the human race with and count the centuries down one after another and you will find that Hell is a VERY CROWDED PLACE! And the Easy Believe Gospel fills it even more by the hour!

I don't think many in our churches today truly understand what true conversion is. I believe this is because the real Gospel isn't preached much anymore. Therefore, multitudes have joined the church with an empty religious profession and a faith that is no more substantive than a hole in the wall. Many ministers themselves are as lost as a goose in a snowstorm, so how can they point a sinner to Christ savingly when they have never found that out for themselves?

We live in a day of an unconverted ministry, an apostate church, and a false Gospel. How can anyone get truly saved today under such spiritual dryness and deadness? Thankfully, *"Salvation is of the Lord"* (Jonah 2:9). Are men saved by a decision they make or by the supernatural work of the Spirit of God through regeneration? We must examine ourselves to see if we are truly saved:

> *"Examine yourselves, whether ye be in the faith; prove your own selves. Know ye not your own selves, how that Jesus Christ is in you, except ye be reprobates"?* (II Corinthians 13:5)

What is conversion? Is it a physical response to an evangelist's emotional appeal? Does one get saved by walking an aisle or repeating a prayer? Is there a difference between mere mental ascent to the Gospel message and a true heart change? Is there such a thing as a lost religious person? We will look at what conversion means from two well-known figures of the 18th century: John Wesley and George Whitefield. Both of these men were once lost religious men who relied on religious duties and exercises to prove their religion. But at the time both of these men were completely lost and unsaved individuals, although on the outside they were busy Christian workers. John Wesley sailed to America, to Georgia as a missionary to the Indians and his time there was a hopeless failure—even being run out of town by the local sheriff! On the ship back to England, Wesley wrote in his journal, "I came to America to save the heathen, but who, will save me?" John Wesley had a group of young students at Oxford University who met with him on a weekly basis to pray, fast, read Scripture, and sing Psalms. They were known around campus for their methodical religion—hence the name the Methodists. Wesley named his group "the Holy Club" for their serious devotions and exercises to God. But the trouble was several of them were entirely unsaved and lost including John Wesley the leader of the group!

John Wesley's conversion experience is worth being familiar with as it shows how a lost religious person can get saved. Here is John Wesley account of that particular evening from his journal dated, 24 May 1738:

"In the evening I went very unwilling to a society in Aldersgate Street, where one was reading Luther's Preface to the Epistle to the Romans. About a quarter before nine, while he was describing the change which God works in the heart through faith in Christ, I felt my heart strangely warmed. I felt I did trust in Christ, Christ alone for salvation, and an assurance was given me that he had taken away my sins, even mine, and saved me from the law of sin and death." We all know what God did with John Wesley after that! John Wesley is quoted as saying: "Give me one hundred men who fear nothing but God, and hate nothing but sin, and I will shake the gates of hell."

And he did just that!

Wesley's good friend and fellow student, George Whitefield was a member of Wesley's Holy Club. George Whitefield took his religious exercises to the extreme by denying himself warm clothing in the winter and good food. He would fast often, pray all night, visit the prisoners in prison, visit the widows, give alms to the poor, but George Whitefield was at this time in his life a lost religious person. It wasn't until his good friend Charles

Wesley loaned him a book written by the Scotsman, Henry Scougal, *entitled "The Life of God in the Soul of Man"* that Whitefield was converted. The words of Scougal gripped his heart and conscience, "Do I have the life of God in the soul of man?" he asked himself and he realized he did not. He did not know what it was like to be Born Again. Shortly thereafter, Whitefield gave his life to Christ and was soundly converted and God used Whitefield to shake two continents for God in revival! George Whitefield's message was *"Ye Must Be Born Again!"*

When Jesus was here in His earthly ministry as He went about into towns and villages, those who encountered Him experienced CHANGE. Let me ask you friend. "Have you experienced change? Is the reality of God real in your own life? Do you know the life of God in the soul of man? Or do you just stand on an old profession of faith and a long track record of service? Ye must be born again!

We now will begin to describe and demonstrate what the true biblical Gospel is by presenting a God-centered Gospel. God saves a lost person for His glory not for man's happiness. The modern church has taken salvation out of the hands of God and placed it in the hands of men but salvation is of the Lord! If you are saved friend, it is because God gave you saving faith:

"For by grace are ye saved through faith; and that not of yourselves: it is the gift of God: not of works, lest any man should boast" (Ephesians 2:8-9).

The Puritans preached a God-centered Gospel. Jonathan Edwards and George Whitefield preached a God-centered Gospel. John and Charles Wesley preached a God-centered Gospel. Charles Spurgeon preached a God-centered Gospel—and revival followed all these men! A God-centered Gospel centers around the glory of God. A man-centered Gospel centers on the happiness of man—which is mere humanism! Let us examine the great doctrines of the Gospel:

REPENTANCE:

The first message of the Gospel is "Repent!" All one has to do is study his Bible and see what was preached in the New Testament. Let's take a look and see:

John the Baptist preached repentance.

"And he came into all the country about Jordan, preaching the baptism of repentance for the remission of sins" (Luke 3:3).

Also we read,

"O generation of vipers, who hath warned you to flee from the wrath to

some? Bring forth therefore fruits worthy of repentance" (Luke 3:7-8).

Jesus preached repentance.

"Now after that John was put in prison, Jesus came into Galilee, preaching the gospel of the kingdom of God. And saying, The time is fulfilled, and the kingdom of God is at hand: repent ye, and believe the gospel" (Mark 1:14,15).

The Gospel of Jesus was a call to repentance!

"I tell you, Nay: but, except ye repent, ye shall all likewise perish" (Luke 13:3).

What did Jesus' disciples preach? "And they went out, and preached that men should repent" (Mark 6:12). And we see also in the Book of Acts what the early church preached, "Then Peter said unto them, Repent and be baptized every one of you in the name of Jesus Christ for the remission of sins" (Acts 2:38).

What did the Apostle Paul preach?

"Testifying both to the Jews, and also to the Greeks, repentance toward God, and faith toward our Lord Jesus Christ" (Acts 20:21).

As the Apostle Paul stood before King Agrippa he preached the Gospel to him,

> *"Whereupon, O king Agrippa, I was not disobedient unto the heavenly vision: but showed first unto them of Damascus, and at Jerusalem, and throughout all the coasts of Judea, and then to the Gentiles, that they should repent and turn to God, and do works meet for repentance"* (Acts 26:20).

And when the Apostle Paul addressed the men of Athens he told warned them,

> *"And the times of this ignorance God winked at: but now commandeth all men everywhere to repent"* (Acts 17:30).

But why should men repent? Because God is a God who must punish sin and all men are born in sin. We see how God views the unrepentant sinner,

> *"God judgeth the righteous, and God is angry with the wicked every day. If he turn not, he will whet his sword; he hath bent his bow, and made it ready"* (Psalm 7:11,12).

God stands behind the unrepentant sinner with a raised sword ready to cut him down. This is the Gospel of Spiritual Awakenings and revivals.

That God is both a God of love and a God of justice. And what is love but love toward sinful man to warn him of his danger! To call a person to repentance is to love them by warning them to flee impending danger! If a bridge was out in a rain storm and a car was approaching and you stood waving your arms and hollering at the car's driver not to proceed any further because it was certain death. He would be grateful to you for saving his life and the life of his family. By standing and waving your arms and shouting at the top of your lungs, STOP! STOP! STOP! You kept the car from plunging into the icy water below. That is the purpose of the first message of the Gospel: Repent! To avoid damnation in a Devil's Hell! If you don't repent you'll surely go to Hell, even if you are the chairman of the deacons!

God has provided a substitute for sin in the Person of His Son, Christ Jesus. Those who repent and believe on Him are saved. If you are not sick you have no need of a doctor, but is you contract a deadly disease you need a remedy! Jesus Christ is the only remedy for sin! But you must first feel your need of Him. We read this in Luke's Gospel:

> *"And Jesus answering said unto them, they that are whole need not a physician: but they that are sick. I came not to call the righteous, but sinners to repentance"* (Luke 5:31,32).

Notice he said that He called sinners to REPENTANCE. A good study on this is found in the Gospel of Luke in chapter fifteen in the parable of the lost sheep, the lost coin, and the lost son. Notice what God's Word declares about true conversion:

> *"Rejoice with me; for I have found my sheep which was lost. I say unto you, that likewise joy shall be in heaven over one sinner that repenteth, more than over ninety and nine just persons which need no repentance"* (Luke 15:6,7).

Again, in the parable of the lost coin we read:

> *"Rejoice with me; for I have found the piece which I had lost. Likewise, I say unto you there is joy in the presence of the angels of God over one sinner that repenteth"* (Luke 15:9,10).

That begs the question: "Have the angels rejoiced over your repentance? Or did you just join the church and confuse church membership with salvation?"

The "old Gospel" was a God-centered Gospel centered around the glory of God in the salvation of men. We must preach a "high view of God". This is best illustrated by the following story:

REGENERATION

In the 18th century an English gentleman traveled in his carriage to Scotland to hear good preaching. He said that the first preacher he heard opened his text in the Book of Isaiah and preached a God who was high and lifted up! "For thus saith the high and lofty One that inhabiteth eternity, whose name is Holy; I dwell in the high and holy place, with him also that is of a contrite and humble spirit to revive the spirit of the humble, and to revive the heart of the contrite ones" (Isaiah 57:15). This made an impression on the Englishman. Next he went to hear another preacher who chose for his text Jeremiah, "The heart is deceitful above all things, and desperately wicked: who can know it"(Jeremiah 17:9)? The Englishman went away from that sermon with a view of his own black heart. And this startled him. Lastly, he visited an old Scottish preacher who preached on the loveliness of Jesus Christ taking for his text the Gospel of Matthew, "Again the kingdom of heaven is like unto a merchant man, seeking goodly pearls: who, when he had found one pearl of great price, sent and sold all that he had, and bought it" (Matthew 13: 45-46). This wounded the Englishman like a cannon ball! He realized how badly he needed the Lord Jesus who was the Pearl of Great price worth selling all for so He can be gained! On the carriage ride back to his estate in England the man was gloriously saved!

Unfortunately, modern evangelism does not preach such needful doctrines as part of the Gospel. We have replaced sound doctrine with amusing stories and funny jokes to entertain our people as we give them what they want to hear instead of what they need. And Sunday after Sunday they are gospel-hardened on their way to Hell!

Old time preachers were not afraid to call sin black and hell hot! And they warned about a future Judgment that awaited all mankind! They warned me to flee from the wrath to come! They preached the law before grace and thundered about the strictness and severity of God's unbending law and that all men will stand guilty before the Judge of all the earth on That Day because all men will fail that test of their lives compared to the strictness of the law of God "

> *For all have sinned and come short of the glory of God"* (Romans 3:23).

RUIN

As we share the Gospel with others we need to focus on the doctrine of Ruin first and foremost. This is what Jesus did in His encounter with the

Samaritan woman at the well. First, He brought out the fact that she was a big sinner.

> *"Jesus saith unto her, Go, call thy husband, and come hither. The woman answered and said, I have no husband. Jesus said unto her, Thou hast well said, I have no husband. For thou hast had five husbands; and he whom thou now hast is not thy husband: in that saidst thou truly"* (John 4:16-18).

Modern evangelism offers Jesus before people feel their need of Him. We offer our little Jesus to folks and they take him like they would a free stick of chewing gum, and they chew on Him awhile until the flavor goes out of their religion! Jesus said, "For the Son of man is come to seek and to save that which was lost" (Luke 19:10). Before a person can be saved they must get lost! One must feel the guilt and weight of sin to feel the need of a Savior from sin. So the doctrine of Ruin is first and foremost a good place to start with the Gospel. Men must be awakened to their lost condition and their perilous position outside of Christ's Blood!

Men must be shown their danger of dying in their sins and being damned in a Devil's Hell. We must preach searching sermons that allow room for the Spirit of God to work as a hammer to break up any false foundations of a false faith. The Word of God in Jeremiah declares: "Is not my word like as a fire? saith the LORD; and like a hammer that breaketh the rock in pieces" (Jeremiah 23:29)? The false foundation of an empty religious profession must be smashed to pieces! God's Word as a fire must smoke out all false refuges that sinners flee to that are useless to them such as good works and a good reputation. As a fire alarms and awakens, so too our sermons must be awakening messages to arouse sinners out of their slumber to recognize their great danger of being under the condemnation of a Holy God unless there is a change within. And that change is a new nature through faith in Christ Jesus whereby the Spirit of God works a work of grace upon the heart. God's Word in Ezekiel states,

> *"A new heart also will I give you, and a new spirit will I put within you: and I will take away the stony heart out of your flesh, and I will give you a heart of flesh. And I will put my spirit within you, and cause you to walk in my statutes, and ye shall keep my judgments, and do them"* (Ezekiel 36:26,27).

Men must be shown their danger of dying in their sins outside of Christ's Blood. We must ask ourselves a question: "Am I a sinner because I sin? Or do I sin because I am a big sinner?" Our sinful nature will damn us eternally unless we exercise repentance toward God and faith in our Lord Jesus Christ. All men need to be saved. All are born in sin, and all must repent and be converted if they would be saved. Therefore, it is critically important that we do not offer Jesus in the Gospel to those who do not feel their need of Him. To do so is to cast pearls before swine. "Give not that which is holy unto the dogs, neither cast ye your pearls before swine, lest they trample them under their feet, and turn again and rend you" (Matthew 7:6).

Our job as ministers of the Gospel and workers of the Gospel is to first GET MEN LOST, to where they feel their need of a remedy for sin. THEN, point them to the remedy for sin in the Person of Christ Jesus!

REDEMPTION

The heart of the Gospel is the doctrine of Redemption. Christ dying for sinful man. One of the best ways to grasp this doctrine of redemption is to think of the concept of the old marketplace in ancient times. The old marketplace in Bible times was called the Agora. When I visited the ancient ruins of Ephesus, my tour guide took me to the spot within the city that was the marketplace where items were bought and sold. Slaves were bought and sold in the marketplace. This market was called the Agora.

A Greek word for redemption is the word, "agorazzo". Do you see the word "agora" in that word "agorazzo"? Regarding our redemption this is the thought: Jesus paid our sin debt on Calvary and through His death on the Cross He entered the marketplace of sin and purchased us by His Blood. That is our redemption! Jesus paid our penalty for sin by being our substitute for sin.

> *"For Christ also hath once suffered for sins, the just for the unjust, that he might bring us to God, being put to death in the flesh, but quickened by the Spirit"* (1 Peter 3:18).

Christ's death on the Cross not only freed us from the penalty of sin it freed us from the power of sin. Let us look at another word for redemption in the Greek: "ek" means to take out of. If you put that little preposition, "ek" in front of the world "agorazzo" then you have the word, "ek-agorazzo"; which means, Christ not only entered the marketplace of sin and purchased us by His Blood, HE TOOK US OUT of the marketplace of sin freeing us from the power of sin!

The man God uses is a God-called preacher who preaches the Gospel of the Son of God with an anointing of the Spirit of God in preaching "searching sermons."

CHAPTER NINE

THE MAN GOD USES: IS A YIELDED MAN

❖ "Our fruitfulness to God depends on four things:
❖ yieldedness, obedience, holiness, usefulness.
❖ Without yieldedness, there is no obedience;
❖ without obedience, there is no holiness;
❖ without holiness, there is no usefulness."

E. A. Johnston

The man God uses is a yielded man. Yielded to the Word of God. Yielded to the will of God. Yielded to the Spirit of God. Yielded to the Lordship of Jesus Christ. Some believers have a walk with God in which they inform God what they intend to do for Him and then ask God to follow them in blessings. Jesus never said, "I will follow you." Jesus said, "You follow me." To follow someone we must be submissive to them as a soldier would be submissive to a commanding officer. As a student would be submissive to a teacher. As a prisoner would be submissive to a jailer. Each of these speak of the need for yieldedness on the part of the one who is under another in authority. God requires perfection. God requires total obedience. God requires holiness. Thankfully, sinful man has grace given to meet these conditions set by God. Christ in us as believers can do for us what we cannot do for ourselves.

If you truly desire usefulness to God in a life of service to Him, then it is critically important to be yielded to God in all things. We read in Romans chapter six and in verses 12-13:

> *"Let not sin therefore reign in your mortal body, that ye should obey it in the lusts thereof. Neither yield ye your members as instruments of un-righteousness unto sin: but yield yourselves unto God, as those that are alive from the dead, and your members as instruments of righteousness unto God."* (Romans 6:12-13)

We see the word "yield" mentioned twice in that passage. And we see there are two things that can "reign" on the throne of one's heart: self can reign there or Christ can reign there—but there is not room for both. One must go. Like the prophet Elijah addressed the people assembled atop Mt. Carmel for the contest between the prophets of Baal and the Living God:

> *"And Elijah came unto all the people, and said, How long halt ye between two opinions? If the LORD be God,*

follow him: but if Baal, then follow him. And the people answered him not a word" (1 Kings 18: 21*)*.

Self must be dethroned and another must be enthroned—the Lord Jesus Christ. Self must go the way of the Cross. The message of the Cross in the life of a believer is a forgotten doctrine in the modern church. But God has not forgotten it! For He sent His only begotten Son on the behalf of sinful man to come down here so we can go up there; to suffer, die and be buried and to rise again and ascend back into heaven where He not sits at the right hand of the Father and He earned that right by WAY OF A BLOODY CROSS! Christ in His earthly ministry was one hundred percent yielded to the will of God one hundred percent of the time. It was His yieldedness to the will of the Father that led Him to Calvary to die for sinful men.

An example of a man who "was not yielded to God" was King Saul. Unfortunately, the bulk of the Church is comprised by individuals who name the name of Christ but who refuse to yield their daily living to Him in His Lordship. Self is still on the throne and calling the shots and deciding just how God will be served and in what capacity. This was the case of King Saul who was a self-ruled man. God, had given King Saul, by His prophet Samuel, implicit instructions to go to Gilgal to battle the Amalekites.

> *"Now go and smite Amalek, and utterly destroy all that they have, and spare them not; but slay both man and woman, infant and suckling, ox and sheep, camel and ass"* (1 Samuel 15:3).

But King Saul had his own plans regarding the spoil of battle—he decided which choice animals to keep and he spared the life of King Agag. The prophet Samuel arrives at Gilgal and Saul greets him with a boast of victory, "And Samuel came to Saul: and Saul said unto him, Blessed be thou of the LORD: I have performed the commandments of the LORD. And Samuel said,

> *"What meaneth then this bleating of the sheep in mine ears, and the lowing of the oxen which I hear"* (1 Samual 15:13-14)?

We are faced in this striking passage of Scripture a sad picture of a willful king who ends up being dethroned because he refused to yield himself to God! Saul begins to make excuses for his disobedience to God's Word. Saul had determined to serve God in the way he chose and not yield to the will and Word of God in his life. We read in the following:

"And Saul said unto Samuel, Yea, I have obeyed the voice of the LORD, and have gone the way which the LORD sent me, and have brought Agag the king of Amalek, and have utterly destroyed the Amalekites. But the people took of the spoil, sheep and oxen, the chief of the things which should have been utterly destroyed, to sacrifice unto the LORD thy God in Gilgal. And Samuel said, Hath the LORD as great delight in burnt offerings and sacrifices, as in obeying the voice of the LORD? Behold, to obey is better than sacrifice, and to hearken than the fat of rams. For rebellion is as the sin of witchcraft, and stubbornness is as iniquity and idolatry. Because thou has rejected the word of the LORD he hath also rejected thee from being king" (1 Samuel 15:20-23).

Some major observations can be made from this passage of scripture:

1. God places a premium on obedience. God demands obedience from all followers of Him.

2. God sees sin differently than man sees it. Man diminishes the evil of sin and sins easily. God, on the other hand, sees sin from His

perspective in quite a different way. He views all rebellion as witchcraft, which is an abomination before Him. Satan and his angels rebelled against God in heaven and were cast out and those angels are now held in chains of darkness for that rebellion.

3. We should view all sin as a great offense to a holy God and do all we can not to sin or disobey God or His Word.

4. God is looking for followers of His who are "yielded" to Him. The man God uses is a yielded man.

CHAPTER TEN

THE MAN GOD USES IS: A MAN OF BROKENNESS

- ❖ "When God comes in, everything else must go out.
- ❖ God can use an empty cup."

E. A. Johnston

We read in Isaiah 57:15:

"For thus saith the high and lofty One that inhabiteth eternity, whose name is Holy: I dwell in the high and holy place, with him also that is of a contrite and humble spirit, to revive the spirit of the humble, and to revive the heart of the contrite ones" (Isaiah 57:15).

Notice how God views brokenness in His followers. He states that the person who is humble and broken (contrite) is near to Him and has access to Him. The very word "contrite" means to be crushed to powder. Alan Redpath made the statement:

"That before God can use a man He must crush him."

When I took martial arts, my Sifu in Kung Fu asked me if I had any previous training in martial arts. I replied, "No." He said, "That is good. You are an empty cup." Meaning I did not have to be retrained in another discipline. God is looking for "empty cups", empty of self.

I cannot think of any way to better express this doctrine of brokenness than the following story about Sam Jones the evangelist of the 19th century. Sam Jones had a revival ministry that shook America and major cities experienced the power of God in revival and awakening under his mighty ministry. But before Sam Jones entered the ministry, he had been a lawyer in Georgia—a drunk lawyer. At the death bed of his father, Sam Jones gave up booze and soon gave his life to Christ and the Gospel. But before Sam Jones could be used of God in big ways he had to become a broken man. This theme is illustrated in the following story from his life:

Sam was at his home in Cartersville, Ga when he received a telegram from Texas inviting him to go to Southwest Texas to preach to the cowboys. After praying about it he boarded a train and traveled to Texas. For two weeks he preached the gospel of Jesus Christ to the cowboys in Texas. When the meetings ended, the cowboys wanted to give Sam Jones a love offering. They felt the laborer was worthy of his hire and they had been wonderfully blessed for the time Sam had spent among them.

But there was a problem—they had no money, not a single dollar in any of their pockets. They didn't know what to do. Sam Jones returned to Cartersville with no love offering or compensation of any kind.

Several weeks had passed when suddenly one day, Sam received a telegram. It was from the cowboys in Texas, and it read like this: "We are sending you a love offering and we are shipping you a carload of broncos."

Sam Jones scratched his head as he looked in amazement at that telegram. "What am I gonna do," he said, "with a carload of wild horses in the small town of Cartersville?" His friend standing beside him said, "Why, it's very easy, hold an auction sale. Sell the horses and you'll get your money. You can get your love offering and put it in your pocket."

Sam Jones thought it was a good suggestion so when the horses arrived, he held a horse auction. He sold the broncos—all except one. He kept the finest looking bronco for his son. But the son had never in his life been on the back of an unbroken bronco and Sam Jones wondered what he could do. He called the cowboy who had brought the carload of broncos to Cartersville and said, "Will you take this bronco and break him so that my son can ride him?"

"Yes sir," said the cowboy. 'I'd be glad to."

"How much will you charge?"

"Fifteen dollars," said the cowboy.

"Alright," said Sam, "take him away."

The cowboy disappeared with the bronco. Two weeks later he came back. "Is he broken?" asked Sam.

"Yes, sir, he's broken."

"Can my son ride him in perfect safety?"

"Yes, sir. Your son can ride him in perfect safety."

The father thought that before allowing his son to ride the bronco, he'd better mount himself and make sure the cowboy had broken it. As he started toward the horse, the cowboy came running and waving his hands in alarm. "What's the matter?" asked Sam. "What's gone wrong?"

"Oh," said the cowboy, "he's only broken on one side, and you're mounting from the wrong side."

"That will never do. My son might make a mistake and he might mount from the wrong side. How much will you charge to break him on the other side?"

"Fifteen dollars," replied the cowboy.

"Alright," said Sam. "Take him away and break him on the other side."

Another two weeks passed and again the cowboy came back leading the bronco.

"Is he broken?" asked Sam.

"Yes, sir. He's broken."

"Both sides?"

"Yes, sir. Both sides. Your son can ride him in perfect safety from either side."[7]

That story is an excellent illustration of the average Christian. The average Christian, like the bronco, is only broken on one side. He'll do this, but he won't do that. He'll go here, but he won't go there. God cannot use him because God cannot trust or rely upon him. The man God uses is the man who is broken on BOTH SIDES.

---

[7] E. A. Johnston, "Sam Jones, A New Biography" (Florida: Old Paths Publications, 2023) pp 45-48.

CHAPTER ELEVEN

THE MAN GOD USES:
HAS A BURDEN FOR SOULS

- ❖ "I have made up my mind: Even if I have to die, I will preach the Gospel in China. I will die a willing death, if only my fellowmen be saved." John Sung
- ❖ "Sung died at the age of 42 after a fifteen year preaching ministry that shook all of China for God and that had seen over 200,000 souls saved."

E. A. Johnston

When I was sixteen years old, I worked a summer job at a local grocery store and saved that money. Rather than spend it on myself foolishly or selfishly, I wanted to do something special with it. I noticed that there was a busy intersection in my neighborhood where drivers became impatient and honked their horns and shook their fists at one another. One day i also noticed that the bus bench at that intersection had a new sign on it that read: "rent me". The bus bench had previously been used to advertise local businesses like a pizza chain or dry cleaners. I thought it would be a wonderful idea to have a Bible verse painted on that bus bench that drivers could not help but notice as they came to that busy intersection. I went through my Bible and picked out what I felt would be a good verse to help people. I chose Ephesians 4:26,

> *"Be ye angry, and sin not: let not the sun go down upon your wrath."* (Ephesians 4:26)

I paid the $30 deposit and signed a one year contract (at $30 a month) with the bench company to have a painter come and paint Ephesians 4:26 on that bus bench so folks would read it and think of God and think of being kinder to one another and not be so angry at each other. I am looking at a photograph of that bus bench now (picture below), it was taken over fifty years ago; in a big cursive hand is written, *"Let not the Sun Go Down upon your Wrath"* Eph. 4:26. I was just a kid in high school, but even back then I had a burden for the souls of men.

I fell in love with Gospel tracts at an early age. The man who led me to Christ when I was thirteen-years-old, gave me a job in his Bible book store across the alley from where I lived. In the Bible book store were racks of good Gospel tracts. I read every one of them with delight as they told of faraway places and adventure like Eskimos fishing in Alaska to pearl divers in South America. Each story had a theme of salvation and how Jesus died for our sins. I have been handing out Gospel tracts ever since; I give them to police officers, workers on my home, strangers at the mall, servers in restaurants. When I go to MacDonalds, I hand one to the person at the window where I pay, and another to the person that hands me my food. I have always had a tract ministry to tell others about the one who came down here so we can go up there—Jesus Christ. I have gone through neighborhoods, ringing doorbells and knocking on doors to hand out tracts and share the gospel. I believe in proactive evangelism: Jesus never said, "Come and hear" but "go and tell".

When God called me to be His preacher then I went all out in evangelism. I have preached over two thousand sermons proclaiming the Good News of salvation in Christ Jesus. I have had a personal witness for Jesus for years as Proverbs states, "He who wins souls is wise"(Proverbs 11:30). I have written my own gospel tracts and have had them printed up to be handed out. I have gone door to door in neighborhoods witnessing for Jesus. I have witnessed for Christ in homes and hospitals and prisons. Once you're truly saved you cannot wait to tell others about Jesus!

But I believe I have a burden for souls because a man had a burden for my soul. He wouldn't let me go to Hell. There was a pastor who lived across the street from my home and he saw an awkward teenager growing up in a godless, troubled home. He began to pray for me. He had a burden for my soul. One day he invited me over to his house to have Saturday breakfast with his family. As I sat at his kitchen table I saw something I never saw before and heard something I never had heard before. I saw a family bowed in prayer. I heard a prayer made for me. This man wouldn't let me go to Hell: he reached out to me and gave my first Bible; he gave me my first job (in his Bible book store); he invited me to his church; he prayed over me and for me and witnessed Jesus to me until at a revival service I gave my heart to Christ Jesus. I want others to know the joy of knowing Christ Jesus as their Savior.

But there have been times in my life where I failed to witness to others about the Christ of the gospel. His face haunts me still. I was having some construction work done on my house and I hired a three man crew to do roof work and paint. I would meet them at my house around 7am each morning before I went to my office. One of the workers, the youngest of the three, always was the first to arrive. While we waited on the others we would exchange small talk like sports or the weather. Back in those days I made it a habit to read the morning newspaper each day, especially the obituary page. One Saturday morning as I sat drinking my coffee and reading the newspaper I saw a photo of a man stare at me from the top of the page of the obituary section. It was the young construction worker who had been working on my home, he had tragically died suddenly and was only 33 years old. I felt awful. I felt bad because I had failed to witness to this young man. How could I be so spiritually insensitive to him! Looking back on it, obviously God had this young man there at my house first thing, before the other men arrived, as an opportunity for me to share Jesus with him. But I failed miserably in this and now I deeply regretted my disobedience to God in not sharing the Gospel more regularly with others. Since that time I have never failed to press a gospel tract into the hands of any worker who comes to my home and witness for Jesus. That young man's sudden death was a chilling reminder to me to be a more effective witness for Christ within my community.

MAKING USE OF DIVINE APPOINTMENTS TO SHARE THE GOSPEL

There have been times in my life where it was obvious to me that God was working in the life of a person who He strategically put into my path in my day-to-day activities. These "divine appointments" were meant for me to share the Gospel with strangers. I remember driving through Atlanta on the interstate and a police car turned on its lights and pulled me over for a traffic stop. The officer approached my car and informed me I was speeding. I apologized to him and said I was on my way to a preaching engagement out of town and I was so excited to get there I had taken my eyes off the speedometer. He gave me a warning instead of a traffic ticket, but as I spoke to him I felt he was troubled about something. I said to him, "I want to give you something that I know will help you, it has helped me immensely." And I reached into my glove box and handed him a pocket Bible. He thanked me for it and promised me he would read it. I felt God had this police officer pull me over so I could give him a bible.

As we go about our daily routine it is important for us to keep our "spiritual antennas" up to see where and with whom God would have us share the "Good News" of His Son Jesus! Be sure to keep a few extra pocket Bibles in your car to give away, and be sure to have a ready supply of favorite gospel tracts to hand out as you go. For the man God uses is a man who has a burden for the souls of men.

CHAPTER TWELVE

THE MAN GOD USES:
IS THE MAN WHO OBEYS HIM

❖ "Absolute surrender means absolute dependence."

E. A. Johnston

God looks for faith. God demands obedience. The man God uses is the man who obeys God and obeys the Word of God. Let us take a look at a few men in our bible who were obedient to God. God told Noah to build an ark and he did just that and he did it to specifications. Noah had to have faith to believe God to build the ark; but he had to obey God to build the ark. We see this in the following passage of Scripture:

> *"And God looked upon the earth, and, behold, it was corrupt: for all flesh had corrupted his way upon the earth. And God said unto Noah, The end of all flesh is come before me; for the earth is filled with violence through them; and, behold, I will destroy them with the earth. Make thee an ark of gopher wood; rooms shalt thou make in the ark, and shalt pitch it within and without with pitch. And this is the*

fashion which thou shalt make if of: The length of the ark shall be three hundred cubits, the breadth of it fifty cubits, and the height of it thirty cubits. A window shalt thou make to the ark, and in a cubit shalt thou finish it above; and the door of the ark shalt thou set in the side thereof; with lower, second, and third stories shalt thou make it.

"And, behold, I, even I, do bring a flood of waters upon the earth, to destroy all flesh, wherein is the breath of life, from under heaven; and every thing that is in the earth shall die. But with thee will I establish my covenant; and thou shalt come into the ark, thou, and thy sons, and thy wife, and thy son's wives with thee. And of every living thing of all flesh, two of every sort shalt thou bring into the ark, to keep them alive with thee; they shall be male and female. Of fowls after their kind, and of cattle after their kind, of every creeping thing of the earth after its kind, two of every sort shall come unto thee, to keep them alive. And take thou unto thee of all food that is eaten, and thou shalt gather it to thee; and it shall be for food for thee, and for them. Thus did Noah, according to all that

God commanded him, so did he" (Genesis 6:12-22).

Notice that the last verse is the "obedience verse". Noah obeyed God completely of all God had commanded him. And this should be the case with us as well friends! God places a premium on obedience to Him. We see this truth all throughout the Word of God. God is a God who places a high premium on obedience to Him.

"And Samuel said, Hath the LORD as great delight in burnt offerings and sacrifices, as in obeying the voice of the LORD. Behold, to obey is better than sacrifice, and to hearken than the fat of rams" (1 Samuel 15:22).

Abraham is known for being a man of faith, but his faith was demonstrated because of his obedience. We read in Genesis 22:18,

"And in thy seed shall all the nations of the earth be blessed; because thou has obeyed my voice."

Christ was obedient to the will of the Father in His submission to the Cross. We read in Hebrews:

"Who in the days of his flesh, when he had offered up prayers and supplications with strong crying and tears unto him that was able to save him from death, and was heard in that

he feared. Though he were a Son, yet learned he obedience by the things which he suffered" (Hebrews 5:7-8).

As Christians we must follow a crucified Christ in a life of discipleship. A disciple is a learner who is obedient to his Master. Jesus placed an emphasis upon obedience to those who followed Him.

"Then said Jesus unto his disciples, If any man will come after me, let him deny himself, and take up his cross, and follow me. For whosoever will save his life shall lose it: and whosoever will lose his life for my sake shall find it" (Matthew 16:24-25).

Again and again, Jesus drilled it into His men the importance of obedience as a follower of His. He taught against mere lip service to Him,

"Not every one that saith unto me, Lord, Lord, shall enter into the kingdom of heaven but he that doeth the will of my Father which is in heaven" (Matthew 7:21).

One's devotion to Christ was to be displayed by love and obedience to Him. In the Gospel of John we read, "Jesus answered and said unto him, If a man love me, he will keep my words, and my Father will love him, and we will come unto him, and make our abode with him" (John 14:23).

There is a tendency to fall into Antinomianism (anti-against; nomos-law). Where one believes he or she can be a Christian and still hang onto their sins. This is a dangerous and erroneous doctrine. Jesus never preached a sinning religion! We should each heed the word of God which declares,

> *"And being made perfect, he became the author of eternal salvation unto all them THAT OBEY HIM"* (Hebrews 5:9, emphasis mine).

The man God uses is the man who obeys Him.

CHAPTER THIRTEEN

THE MAN GOD USES: BELIEVES IN A DYNAMITE GOD WHO DOES SUPER-DUPER THINGS!

❖ "If we served such a dynamite God, then how come so many of us live firecracker lives?"

Vance Havner

I believe the words of Vance Havner are both compelling and convicting. We must ask ourselves the question: Why did the early church displayed in the Book of Acts have such incredible influence and power that it was said of them,

> *"These that have turned the world upside down are come hither also"* (Acts 17:6).

Why is our brand of modern-day Christianity so anemic and uninfluential? Why does the church in America today lack power? I believe the answers lies in the sad fact that the church found out a long time ago they could get more done faster by money and manpower; but in former times the church operated on prayer and Holy Ghost power!

It all boils down to the fact that many today just do not "believe" in the God of the Bible but in a god our own imagination. Our god wouldn't send anybody to Hell. Even though Jesus stated quite the opposite,

> *"And fear not them which kill the body, but are not able to kill the soul: but rather fear him which is able to destroy both soul and body in hell"* (Matthew 10:28).

Many in the church today have gotten out their pocketknives and have carved out a god for themselves that won't get in the way of their daily living. They want to have a hope of heaven and still hug their favorite sins. We don't believe in a God who works miracles today. We feel that was for "back then" and "not now". But God is still the same God and He has not changed His stripes.

> *"For I am the LORD. I change not; therefore ye sons of Jacob are not consumed. Even from the days of your fathers ye are gone away from mine ordinances, and have not kept them. Return unto me, and I wil return unto you, saith the LORD of hosts"* (Malachi 3:6-7).

It is our own lack of faith, our unbelief that hinders both God and us and keeps us from receiving blessings from the Lord. We see this is so in the Gospel of Matthew, *"And he did not many mighty works there because of their unbelief"* (Matthew 13:58). Some so-called Christians don't believe in the miracles of the Bible. Sam Jones the evangelist said, "I would believe my Bible if it said that Jonah swallowed the whale!"

If we read our Bibles we will find that it is the individuals who "believed God" was able were also the ones who saw God move in miraculous ways and it increased their faith to be even more bold for God!

Joshua was a man who took God at His Word. God said Jericho would fall if the people did such and such. They did such and such and Joshua exclaimed,

> *"And it came to pass at the seventh time, when the priests blew with the trumpets, Joshua said unto the people, Shout; for the LORD hath given you the city"* (Joshua 6:16).

Joshua was a man of God who believed in a dynamite God who did super duper things! And he believed in setting up memorials to God so other generations would believe in the mighty God as well. We get a sense of this from the following passage of Scripture:

"And the people came up out of Jordan on the tenth day of the first month, and encamped in Gilgal, in the east border of Jericho. And those twelve stones, which they took out of Jordan, did Joshua pitch in Gilgal. And he spake unto the children of Israel, saying, When your children shall ask their fathers in time to come, saying, What mean these stones? Then ye shall let your children know, saying, Israel came over this Jordan on dry land. For the LORD your God dried up the waters of Jordan from before you, until ye were passed over, as the LORD your God did to the Red sea, which he dried up from before us, until we were gone over. That all the people of the earth might know the hand of the LORD, that is mighty: that ye might fear the LORD your God forever" (Joshua 4:19-24).

The faith of Joshua was so strengthened and emboldened that he could look up to his God and believe with all his heart that God could perform "all things" no matter how difficult or hard. We get a sense of his incredible faith in a dynamite God as in the heat of battle he asks God to stop the sun and make it stand still!

"Then spake Joshua to the LORD in the day when the LORD delivered up the Amorites before the children of Israel, and he said in the sight of Israel, Sun, stand thou still upon Gibeon; and thou, Moon, in the valley of Ajalon. And the sun stood still and the moon stayed, until the people had avenged themselves upon their enemies. Is not this written in the book of Jasher? So the sun stood thill in the midst of heaven, and hasted not to go down about a whole day. And there was no day like that before it or after it, that the LORD hearkened unto the voice of a man: for the LORD fought for Israel" (Joshua 10:12-14).

The man God uses believes in the God of the Bible and the man God uses is the man who believes in a dynamite God who does super duper things!

CHAPTER FOURTEEN

THE MAN GOD USES:
IS A MAN OF REVIVAL

❖ "In 1740 when God moved through New England it was called 'The Great Awakening'. Revival has often been referred to as 'an awakening'. At Gethsemane Jesus faced the 'crises point' of His earthly ministry and His disciples slept right through it. Today the church is in a 'crises point' and we are sleeping right through it."

E. A. Johnston

The man God uses is a man of revival. It is a sad fact that if a real revival of religion appeared on the scene today few would recognize it and many would fight against it. Very few pastors have studied the history of revival and spiritual awakening in any depth. They merely have a surface knowledge of it and therefore will repeat myths about it, which are actually harmful to it. One such myth is the fable that in 1828 in Albany, New York, 100,000 souls were saved under the ministry of Charles Grandison Finney. This "myth" is a favorite among pastors and preachers who love numbers. But those who quote such nonsense have never taken the time to read or study Finney's own "Memoirs" (which are over 700 pages in length) in which Finney himself states the number of souls converted in that revival in Albany, New York in 1828 was 800 to possible 1,000 out of a population of 9,800 inhabitants. The error and myth of the 100,000 converts attributed to Finney in one town is due to an erroneous entry in a Finney biography by a secular historian; who, mistook the comments of Lyman Beecher (a minister at the time who knew Finney and who first opposed him!) and said they were Finney's converts from his time in Albany, New York in 1828. However, the truth is that Lyman Beecher in a letter to a friend had written he believed the entire converts of the time known as the Second Great Awakening was a figure around 100,000 under a number of combined ministers. It was said of Asahel Nettleton that he had seen 30,000 converts in his mighty revival ministry that covered New England at the time.

The man that God uses is a man of revival, or better stated: a student of revival. It is critically important that we study how God has moved in former times in periods of revival so we may know how to pray, preach and anticipate revival in our day.

I highly recommend the study of the time periods of revival in history. Become familiar with the human instruments who were used in the revivals. Was prayer a factor in the revival appearing? Who were the instruments of prayer? In the revival on the Isle of Lewis in the Scottish Hebrides of 1949-1942 under the preaching of Duncan Campbell; the human prayer instruments used to bring revival to the island were the elderly Smith sisters, one was lame and the other was blind. But they prayed and received visions of a coming revival, they even saw a vision of Duncan Campbell coming to the island!

Make it a point to study the time period known as the Great Awakening in America under Jonathan Edwards and George Whitefield as the primary leaders of that revival. Learn the names and contribution of the other ministers involved in that revival: men like Thomas Prince, Jonathan Parsons, Gilbert Tennent, Joseph Sewall, and a host of others.

Make it a point to study the time period in America known as the Second Great Awakening where the leaders of that revival were: Asahel Nettleton (who was the primary leader) and Charles Finney (who was the secondary leader), as well as the other ministers who were involved in those revivals, men like Lyman Beecher, Noah Porter (pastor of the church in Farmington, Conn) Thomas Shepherd (pastor in Lenox, Mass, the church on the hill), and a host of other worthy men whom God used during that spiritual awakening.

Study the revival of religion in England under John and Charles Wesley and George Whitefield. Study the life of Howell Harris and the evangelical revival in Wales.

Study the 1904 Revival in Wales and the human instrument of that revival: Evan Roberts.

Study the life and ministry of the Chinese evangelist, John Sung, whom God used to shake China with revival between the first and second World Wars.

Study the Cambuslang Revival in Cambuslang, Scotland under the ministry of William McCulloch and George Whitefield.

I have devoted four decades of my life studying revival and the history of revival. I have written over twenty books on the subject of revival. My Ph.D. dissertation was on the revival of religion under Wesley and Whitefield in England. I have over 2,000 revival sermons on SermonAudio.com. The point I am trying to make is that it takes TIME and DEDICATION TO STUDY REVIVAL. Men who I have known who are men of revival have dedicated their entire lives to its study: men like Richard Owen Roberts, Iain Murray, Stephen Olford, Ted Rendall, J. I. Packer.

The man God uses is a man of revival. Men like these:

"The Apostle Paul, Luther, Wesley, Whitefield, Knox, Edwards, Finney, Spurgeon, Moody…each shared a common denominator, a fire in their belly. They were each so eaten up with the Gospel and thirsty for Christ and filled with the Holy Ghost they could not stand idly by while others perished. They saw nothing but eternity, worshipped a Holy God, and served a Risen Christ; living not for earth nor its gains but living only for heaven and its rewards. When they preached, they linked the Devil with sin and the Cross with salvation.

They preached hell and its fire and Christ and Him crucified. Not one of them feared King, Queen, or Pope; and not one of them sought the compliments of men." E. A. Johnston

CHAPTER FIFTEEN

THE MAN GOD USES: IS A MAN WHO FINISHES WELL

❖ "Satan came against Jesus at the entrance and exit of His earthly ministry; if the Devil can't get you in the beginning, he will try to get you in the end. Sadly, some promising believers end up with a sad ending, a ruined testimony and a wrecked ministry."

E. A. Johnston

I want us to study a true story about a good king who did a lot of good for God but he ended up with a sad ending. He did not finish well. I believe a tarnished testimony can wipe out all the good that one has done for God and the Gospel. A tarnished testimony can bring dishonor to the cause of Christ and harm to the church of God. A tarnished testimony can hurt the entire body of Christ, as all will feel the pain of one who falls morally at the end and becomes a disgrace to God. Prominent ministries, at times, can end up on an ash heap of moral failure. If one were to research the germination of the ruined testimony, the breakdown begins in the daily quiet time with God and the root is usually pride. An older man wants to feel young and viral again so he takes sexual risks that are off limits to him as a Christian. Or, he over-steps his role under God and reaches for a forbidden thing that displeases the Lord. When a leader falls it should be a lesson to all of us.

"Wherefore let him that thinketh he standeth take heed lest he fall" (1 Corinthians 10:12).

The man God uses is a man who finishes well. Finishing well is hard to do. There are many who don't finish well. I personally have known Christians who had powerful testimonies for Christ and the Gospel, end up crashing and burning in the flames of adultery or suicide. We must be on the watch continually,

"Lest Satan should get an advantage of us: for we are not ignorant of his devices" (2 Corinthians 2:11).

Sam Jones, the greatly used evangelist of the 19th century, was a recovered alcoholic. God used him in mighty revivals all over America, turning major cities like Chicago, Boston, St. Louis, and Nashville upside down for God and the Gospel. Sam Jones had started out as a lawyer in Georgia with a drinking problem. At his father's deathbed he gave up alcohol and soon after was gloriously saved and placed into the preaching ministry with the Methodist Church. Soon, the name Sam Jones was a household word all over America, with hundreds of thousands being converted to Christ through his powerful preaching. But a few months before he suddenly died at the age of 58 while on a train bound for Georgia, he was in a western town and as he passed a saloon he was almost overcome with "the old urge." He ran to his hotel and locked himself in his hotel room and stayed there in prayer until the urge left him. Satan had done his best to ruin Sam Jones at the end but God interposed and kept him.

I want us to study the life of a good king who did much good for God for a long period of time but who, at the end, finished poorly with a sad ending. Let this story be a warning to us all! To get the meaning of our story we must familiarize ourselves with a certain passage of Scripture, in 2 Chronicles, chapter twenty- six. We will study the life of good King Uzziah. Here now is the Word of God:

> *"Then all the people of Judah took Uzziah, who was sixteen years old, and made him king in the room of his father Amaziah. He built Eloth, and restored it to Judah, after that the king slept with his fathers. Sixteen years old was Uzziah when he began to*

reign, and he reigned fifty and two years in Jerusalem. His mother's name also was Lecoliah of Jerusalem. And he did that which was right in the sight of the LORD, according to all that his father Amaziah did.

"And he sought God in the days of Zechariah, who had understanding in the visions of God: and as long as he sought the LORD, God made him to prosper" (2 Chronicles 26:1-5).

Take notice friends, that the statement, *"and as long as he sought the LORD, God made him to prosper"*. This was the key to his success. This was also his downfall when he ceased to seek God and became a self-reliant king. Let us take a look at all the good this good king Uzziah did in the name of God during his lengthy fifty two year reign as king of Judah.

"And he went forth and warred against the Philistines, and brake down the wall of Gath, and the wall of Jabneh, and the wall of Ashdod, and built cities about Ashdod, and among the Philistines. And God helped him against the Philistines, and against the Arabians that dwelt in Gur-ball, and the Mehunims. And the Ammonites gave gifts to Uzziah: and

his name spread abroad even to the entering in of Egypt, for he strengthened himself exceedingly. Moreover Uzziah built towers in Jerusalem at the corner gate, and at the valley gate, and at the turning of the wall, and fortified them. Also he built towers in the desert and digged many wells: for he had much cattle, both in the low country, and in the plains: husbandmen also, and vine dressers in the mountains, and in Carmel: for he loved husbandry.

"Moreover Uzziah had an host of fighting men, that went out to war by bands, according to the number of their account by the hand of Jeiel the scribe and Maaseiah the ruler, under the hand of Hananiah, one of the king's captains.

"The whole number of the chief of the fathers of the mighty men of valour were two thousand and six hundred. And under their hand was an army, three hundred thousand and seven thousand and five hundred, that made war with mighty power, to help the king against the enemy.

"And Uzziah prepared for them throughout all the host shields, and

spears, and helmets, and habergeons, and bows, and slings to cast stones. And he made in Jerusalem engines, invented by cunning men, to be on the towers and upon the bulwarks, to shoot arrows and great stones withal. And his name spread far abroad; for he was marvellously helped, till he was strong.

"But when he was strong, his heart was lifted up to his destruction: for he transgressed against the LORD his God, and went into the temple of the LORD to burn incense upon the altar of incense." Notice how as his heart was lifted up so was his pride. It is his willful pride that gets him to sin and transgress against God Almighty.

"And Azariah the priest went in after him, and with him fourscore priests of the LORD, that were valiant men. And they withstood Uzziah the king, and said unto him, It appertaineth not unto thee, Uzziah, to burn incense unto the LORD, but to the priests the sons of Aaron, that are consecrated to burn incense: go out of the sanctuary, for thou hast trespassed; neither shall it

be for thine honour from the LORD God.

"Then Uzziah was wroth, and had a censer in his hand to burn incense: and while he was wroth with the priests, the leprosy even rose up in his forehead before the priests in the house of the LORD, from beside the incense altar.

"And Azariah the chief priest, and all the priests, looked upon him, and, behold, he was leprous in his forehead, and they thrust him out from thence; yea, himself hasted also to go out, because the LORD had smitten him.

"And Uzziah the king was a leper unto the day of his death, and dwelt in a several house, being a leper; for he was cut off from the house of the LORD: and Jotham his son was over the king's house, judging the people of the land.

"Now the rest of the acts of Uzziah, first and last, did Isaiah the prophet, the son of Amoz, write. So Uzziah slept with his fathers, and they buried him with his fathers in the field of the burial which belonged to the kings; for

they said, He is a leper: and Jotham his son reigned in his stead" (2 Chronicles 26: 1-23).

So here we have the story of the good king who had a sad ending. Of all the good that good king Uzziah accomplished in his long life and long reign of fifty-two years, all that is remembered of him by the people who knew him was in the last comment by them, "He is a leper." All the good he had done was erased because of his disobedience to God because of his self-reliance and his pride which was so extended that he just wasn't satisfied being king, he wanted to be priest as well! And he took it upon himself to act as priest and it cost him dearly. They might as well have put on his headstone only the words, "He is a leper." That was his legacy.

Finishing well is a hallmark of a man used of God. A man faithful to God. A man obedient to God. And a man who walks closely with God right up to the very end. The man God uses is the man who finishes well.

CHAPTER SIXTEEN

THE MAN GOD USES: IS WILLING TO GO OUT ON A LIMB FOR GOD

❖ "Once you step out by faith and get a taste of the supernatural, like Peter, and walk on the water with God—the last thing you want to do is to go back to the safety of the boat."

E. A. Johnston

The man God uses is a man who is willing to stick his neck out for God and the Gospel, even if it means it will get chopped off! The early church thrived because she was hotly persecuted. If the Romans or the Jews killed off some Christians, twenty more appeared in their place ready to go to the death for God and His glory and Christ and His gospel! God loves a challenge. God loves to be proved. God loves it when a man takes the Word of God and stands on it when he has nothing else left to stand upon. God loves it when a man is so helpless, so tried and tired, and beaten and weak, that his only strength is beyond himself because he has cast himself upon Christ the Savior. God loved C. T. Studd. Charles Studd was a young cricketeer, famous throughout all England for his athletic prowess and dignified background being the son of the millionaire gentleman, Edward Studd and of whose vast country estate, Tetworth, was legendary for its champion race horses. C. T. Studd was to inherit his father's fortune but becoming a Christian he gave it all away for Christ and the Gospel and lived by faith the rest of his life as a missionary, first to China, then to India, and finally, to Africa where he died. He lived in total privation in the African bush, separated from his wife and daughters, only separated to God and the Gospel for the sake of the souls of the Africans. C. T. Studd was a man willing to risk all for Christ. Listen to some of his sayings:

> "Christ does not want nibblers of the possible, but grabbers of the impossible."

> "Funds are low again, hallelujah! That means God trusts us and is willing to leave His reputation in our hands."

> "Christ's call is to save the lost, not the stiff-necked; He came not to call scoffers but sinners to repentance; not to build and furnish comfortable chapels, churches, and cathedrals at home in which to rock Christian professors to sleep by means of clever essays, stereotyped prayers, and artistic musical performances, but to capture men from the devil's clutches

and the very jaws of Hell. This can be accomplished only by a red-hot, unconventional, unfettered devotion, in the power of the Holy Spirit, to the Lord Jesus Christ."

"Some want to live within the sound of church and chapel bell, I want to run a rescue shop, within a yard of hell."

"When we are in hand-to-hand conflict with the world, the flesh, and the devil himself, neat little Biblical con-fectionery is like shooting lions with a pea-shooter; God needs a man who will let go and deliver blows right and left as hard as he can hit, in the power of the Holy Ghost. Nothing but forked-lightning Christians will count."

"Only one life,

Twill soon be past;

Only what's done

For Christ will last."

C. T. Studd

The man God uses is the man who is willing to risk it all for Christ and the Gospel come Hell or high water! The early Church had a fire and they turned the world upside down because they loved Christ more than their own skins. They refused to say,

"Caesar is Lord" in the face of punishment and death; they would only say, "Jesus is Lord" no matter the cost or consequence.

The vital Christianity of the early Church should shame us worldly Christians today. The man God uses is the man willing to go out on a limb for God.

CHAPTER SEVENTEEN

THE MAN GOD USES: IS A STUDENT OF REVIVAL

❖ "Ignorance of how God has moved in former times and indifference to the men whom God has used creates shallow Christians who know just enough to be dangerous."

E. A. Johnston

The following list of recommended books on revival is meant to encourage the reading and study of historical revivals. It is by no means comprehensive and these books are merely mentioned to whet the appetite of the serious student of revival.

RECOMMENDED READING LIST ON BOOKS ABOUT REVIVAL

"An Annotated Bibliography of Revival Literature" Richard Owen Roberts

"Revival" Richard Owen Roberts

"Revival" Martyn Lloyd-Jones

"Heart Cry for Revival" Stephen F. Olford

"Fire In The Church" Ted Rendall

"In the Day of Thy Power" Arthur Wallis

"Revival and Revivalism" Iain Murray

"The Cambuslang Revival" Arthur Fawcett

"Channel of Revival: Biography of Duncan Campbell" Andrew Woolsey

"The Journal Once Lost: Diary of John Sung" Levi

"Memoirs of Charles Grandison Finney" Rosell and Dupuis

"Life and Diary of David Brainerd" Jonathan Edwards

"A Faithful Narrative of the Surprising Work of God" Jonathan Edwards

"Sermon: Sinners in the Hands of an Angry God" Jonathan Edwards

"Glory Filled The Land: A Trilogy on the Welsh Revival 1904-1905" Lewis, Morgan, Neprash

"Revival Trilogy" E. A. Johnston

"Sam Jones: A New Biography" E. A. Johnston

"George Whitefield: A Definitive Biography (Volumes one and two) E. A. Johnston

"Asahel Nettleton: Revival Preacher" E. A. Johnston

CHAPTER EIGHTEEN

SOME OF THE BOOKS BY E. A. JOHNSTON

Many of the following books may be purchased individually or as a set by going to Dr. Johnston's webpage in the bookstore at The Old Paths Publications that has links to distributors. Go to:

www.theoldpathspublications.com/Pages/Authors/Johnston.htm

or

Email us: TOP@theoldpathspublications.com

1. *"A Heart Awake: The Authorized Biography of J. Sidlow Baxter"* Foreword by Adrian Rogers (The Old Paths Publications, www.theoldpathspublications.com).
2. *"Realities Of Revival"* Foreword by Stephen F. Olford (Gospel Folio Press, Canada; 2005).
3. *"No Turning Back"* (Gospel Folio Press, Canada; 2005).
4. *"The Master's Plan: Unfolding God's Blueprint For Your Life"* (Gospel Folio Press, Canada; 2006).
5. *"Know The Book: Bible Survey At A Glance"* (Gospel Folio Press, Canada; 2007).

6. *"Jua Kitabu: Tazamo la Biblia"* Know The Book translated into the Swahili by missionary G. I. Harlow (Everyday Publications, Canada; 2007).

7. *"Walking With God"* Foreword by Ted S. Rendall (Gospel Folio Press, Canada; 2007).

8. *"Return To Me: Entering A Right Relationship With God"* (Gospel Folio Press, Canada; 2007).

9. *"Are You In The Book Of Life?"* (Gospel Folio Press, Canada; 2008).

10. *"Call To Revival"* Foreword By Colin Peckham (Gospel Folio Press, Canada; 2008).

11. *"The Church In Revival"* Foreword By Richard Owen Roberts (Gospel Folio Press, Canada; 2008).

12. *"Olford On Scroggie: Stephen Olford's Notes on the Sermon Outlines of Graham Scroggie"* Co-authored with Stephen Olford (The Old Paths Publications: www.theoldpathspublications.com).

13. *"George Whitefield A Definitive Biography, Volumes 1 and 2 Combined"* (The Old Paths Publications: www.theoldpathspublications.com).

14. *"George Whitefield A Definitive Biography In Two Volumes"* (American edition published by Revival Literature, Asheville; 2012).

15. *"God's Hitchhike Evangelist The Biography Of Rolfe Barnard"* Foreword By Bob Doom (The Old

Paths Publications: www.theoldpathspublications.com).

16. *"Asahel Nettleton Revival Preacher"* Foreword By John Thornbury, Preface By Richard Owen Roberts (The Old Paths Publications: www.theoldpathspublications.com).

17. *"Sermons For Revival"* (The Old Paths Publications: www.theoldpathspublications.com).

18. *"A Noble Company Biographical Essays on Notable Particular Baptists in America Volume 11: Portrait of Rolfe Barnard"* (Particular Baptist Press, Springfield; 2018).

19. *"Lectures On Revival For A Laodicean Church,"* (The Old Paths Publications, www.theoldpathspublications.com)

20. *"Sam Jones, A New Biography"* (The Old Paths Publications: www.theoldpathspublications.com)

21. E. A. Johnston's Book Set, (The Old Paths Publications, www.theoldpathspublications.com (30% off retail)

22. "Revival Trilogy, Three Volumes in One": 1. "Realities of Revival," 2. "Call to Revival," 3. "The Church in Revival," The Old Paths Publications, Inc., www.theoldpathspublications.com

23. "How to Have a Dailey Quiet Time," the Old Paths Publications, Inc.,
www.theoldpathspublications.com

24. "Going Higher With God," The Old Paths Publications, Inc.,
www.theoldpathspublications.com

25. "How to Preach For Revival," The Old Paths Publications, Inc.,
www.theoldpathspublications.com

26. "Faith Lessons in A Dynamic God," The Old Paths Publications, Inc.,
www.theoldpathspublications.com

Many of these books can be purchased in The Old Paths Publications Bookstore at a discounted price. Go here:

https://www.theoldpathspublications.com/Pages/BookStore.htm

ABOUT THE AUTHOR

E.A. Johnston in the Outdoor pulpit at Hanham Mount where George Whitefield preached, courtesy of Digby James.

E. A. Johnston, Ph.D., D. B. S., is a Fellow with the Stephen Olford Institute for Biblical Preaching and is an evangelist and author with eighteen published books. He is the founder of Evangelism Awakening, a revival-based ministry whose focus is the study of historical revival and preaching for revival in our day. He has over two thousand sermons on SermonAudio.com.

www.ingramcontent.com/pod-product-compliance
Lightning Source LLC
Chambersburg PA
CBHW071327150726
47997CB00002B/628